"Highly recommended! Andrew Holecek offers readers a rare, semise dreaming. Grasp his hand through the dark descent from the white of the throat, until you reach the blue of the true heart and its secrets."

> —Patricia Garfield, PhD, doctorate in clinical psychology from Temple University; author of the *Los Angeles Times* bestseller, *Creative Dreaming*, translated into seventeen languages; and cofounder of the International Association for the Study of Dreams

"Another brilliant addition to the lucid dreaming canon! This book actually feels more like a workshop than a book, as you are constantly being asked to reflect on your experience and to write notes as you go. A must-read for all who want to learn how to become lucid in their dreams!"

> —Charlie Morley, lucid dreaming teacher, and author of *Dreams of Awakening*

"*The Lucid Dreaming Workbook* provides a spirited collection of Eastern and Western lucid dreaming techniques, along with solid advice for those traveling the lucid dreaming path. If you are wishing to add some Eastern induction methods to your personal repertoire, then you should definitely take a look!"

> —Robert Waggoner, author of *Lucid Dreaming*; and coauthor of *Lucid Dreaming, Plain and Simple*

"Andrew Holecek has written a comprehensive and amazingly interactive manual on how to lucid dream, as well as what to do once you get there. He seamlessly draws from his background in both science and mysticism, citing peer-reviewed journals, the Buddha, and everything in between."

> —Tucker Peck, PhD, clinical psychologist, sleep expert, and meditation teacher

"Andrew Holecek understands practice, and has applied his deep experience to forging a step-by-step path that leads from daily habit and ordinary attention to the magic of lucid dreaming. The easy exercises and clear explanations in this workbook will deepen and enrich the lucid dream adventures of beginners and adepts alike."

—Jennifer Dumpert, author of *Liminal Dreaming*

"*The Lucid Dreaming Workbook* is not for armchair dreamers. No, this is serious nightstand material—the advanced lucid dreaming guide you have been longing for. Not only does Holecek integrate scientific and Eastern perspectives on lucidity with precision and clarity, but he drills into the conflicts that get in the way of a truly advanced lucid dreaming practice. Essential reading for all oneironauts."

—Ryan Hurd, MA, lecturer of psychology at John F. Kennedy University, coeditor of *Lucid Dreaming*, and founder of www.dreamstudies.org

The LUCID DREAMING WORKBOOK

A Step-by-Step Guide to Mastering Your Dream Life

ANDREW HOLECEK

REVEAL PRESS
AN IMPRINT OF NEW HARBINGER PUBLICATIONS

Publisher's Note

Distributed in Canada by Raincoast Books

Copyright © 2020 by Andrew Holecek
         Reveal Press
         An imprint of New Harbinger Publications, Inc.
         5674 Shattuck Avenue
         Oakland, CA 94609
         www.newharbinger.com

Cover design by Sara Christian

Acquired by Jess O'Brien

Edited by Kristi Hein

All Rights Reserved

Library of Congress Cataloging-in-Publication Data

Names: Holecek, Andrew, 1955- author.
Title: The lucid dreaming workbook : a step-by-step guide to mastering your dream life / Andrew Holecek.
Description: Oakland : New Harbinger Publications, 2020. | Includes bibliographical references.
Identifiers: LCCN 2020009212 (print) | LCCN 2020009213 (ebook) | ISBN 9781684035021 (trade paper-
    back) | ISBN 9781684035038 (pdf) | ISBN 9781684035045 (epub)
Subjects: LCSH: Lucid dreams.
Classification: LCC BF1099.L82 H65 2020 (print) | LCC BF1099.L82 (ebook) | DDC 154.6/3--dc23
LC record available at https://lccn.loc.gov/2020009212
LC ebook record available at https://lccn.loc.gov/2020009213

Printed in the United States of America

22   21   20

10   9   8   7   6   5   4   3   2   1   First Printing

For Rose, Vanessa, and Taylor, three generations of love.

Contents

Part I

The Foundations of Lucid Dreaming

Introduction

Welcome to a unique form of night school. Lucid dreaming, which is knowing that you're dreaming while remaining in the dream, offers a form of higher education that is unparalleled in its potential. We spend about two hours every night dreaming, or around 720 hours a year. In the course of an average life, that amounts to some six years. Think about how much you could learn if you had those extra years. It's almost like adding years to your life.

If you're not interested in secondary education but just want to have more fun in your dreams, then welcome to a truly exclusive nightclub. Lucid dreaming, like any form of technology, is neutral. You can do with it what you want. As the following pages reveal, you can use lucid dreaming to fulfill your wildest fantasies. In a lucid dream you become the writer, producer, director, and main actor in an Academy Award–winning production of your own mind. You can have dream sex, race along the French Riviera in a Ferrari, or rip through the Grand Canyon in a fighter jet. Mind becomes reality in a lucid dream, so the only limitation is your imagination.

MY STORY

I have been practicing this art of dreaming for over forty years, covering the entire spectrum of possibilities. Over these decades I've been fortunate enough to study with many of the greatest authorities in the world, both East and West. I've engaged in scientific studies as a subject and conducted studies with cognitive neuroscientists. As a member of the American Academy of Sleep Medicine, I also work with the clinical aspects of sleep. But my ultimate training was during a strict three-year retreat, where I plunged into lucid dreaming in the most rigorous way—and reaped the bountiful fruits of such a deep immersion.

In my early years, I enjoyed the absolute freedom of these special dreams. I looked forward to my dreams the way some people look forward to a night in Las Vegas. And because it was all happening in the privacy of my own mind, what happened in "Vegas" stayed in Vegas.

But one can run riot for only so long, so after a few months I wanted to see if there was more to lucid dreaming than mere entertainment. Instead of indulging my dreams, I started to work with them. It was like adding a fun night shift, adding extra hours in which I could learn about myself using the medium of my dreams and do things I didn't have time for during the day.

The revolutionary discovery of this deeper level of lucid dreaming is that what happens in "Vegas" no longer stays in Vegas. The insights I was gleaning from my lucid dreams were starting to transform my days. I was bringing my rich dream experiences home from my overnight school. Valuable information began to flow in both directions, informing and eventually transforming both waking and dreaming states. Scientists call this "bidirectionality"; it's like opening a two-way street between the dreaming and waking mind, and it's a central theme of our journey in this book. At this deeper level of lucid dreaming, Vegas is replaced with what I call "Vanderbilt," a place of higher learning.

I eventually discovered that lucid dreaming could also be used for spiritual transformation. This is like graduate school or theological seminary, which may not be for everybody. But for those interested in waking up in the spiritual sense, lucid dreaming can develop into *dream yoga*, an ancient spiritual practice that uses the medium of our dreams to explore the nature of mind and reality. Vanderbilt is replaced with the "Vatican," a place for spiritual practice where lucid dreaming leads to enlightenment.

Over many years of nightly practice, I have learned what works and what doesn't in the world of lucid dreaming. If there's a mistake, I've made it. If there's a dead end, I've run into it. But I was determined, and I had an unwavering conviction in the power of this practice. I've had countless lucid dreams and can virtually induce them at will. But I'm not more gifted or special than you. If I can do it, anybody can.

LUCIDITY IN A FLASH

The good news about lucid dreaming is that it just takes one flash of recognition and you're "in." In the blink of an eye, something clicks and you suddenly realize *This is just a dream!* A non-lucid dream instantly transforms into a lucid one. You may have spent your entire life in the "dark," lost in non-lucidity, and then it happens. It's like you've been in a cave, smothered in darkness, for eons. With one flick of a match you can remove a billion years of darkness.

Keeping the light on is a different story. That takes sustained practice. Those who have lucid dreams regularly are those who work at it. Just like any discipline, you will get out of lucid dreaming what you put into it. If you dabble in it, you'll get dabbling results. If you put your heart into it, you'll get dazzling results. I've put my life into it, and I continue to have life-changing results.

HOW TO USE THIS BOOK

For many years I've also been blessed with the opportunity to teach lucid dreaming seminars around the world. Through trial and error and feedback from thousands of students, I have learned what works and what doesn't when it comes to teaching others. In the following pages I share every tip and trick for mastering lucid dreaming. As a dedicated student of science and a lifelong practitioner of meditation, I bring together modern Western knowledge and ancient Eastern wisdom to give you a full-spectrum approach to lucidity.

The live seminars work, so this book follows their successful format. Each chapter presents the necessary information. Then we'll work to digest the material with guided exercises and meditations. Finally, there will be a discussion with commonly asked questions and answers. The most important parts of this book are the exercises and meditations. This is where you'll take the information from your head and bring it into your heart, and eventually into your world.

I encourage you to fully engage in the guided exercises. You will get out of them what you put into them. Writing your experiences in the spaces provided will also help you track your progress and inspire you to go further.

THE POWER OF QUESTIONS

In the spirit of Socrates, questions are often more important than answers. Like a gifted attorney who skillfully leads their witness with pointed questions, the right queries can lead to insight. The most transformative discoveries are made when *you* connect the dots, when *you* come upon insights on your own. Instead of being spoon-fed information, you learn to feed yourself. Those "Aha!" moments are the ones that change you. When the inner light comes on and you utter in amazement, "*Now* I see!" That flash of insight is what you'll remember because you saw it for yourself. The exercises, contemplations, and meditations seeded by questions in the pages ahead are designed to spark that flash.

A non-lucid dream is a "dark" dream, the usual dream when you don't realize that you're dreaming. You're dreaming in the dark, stumbling around and losing your way. A lucid dream is a "lit" dream, a dream in which you can see that you're dreaming. Now you're dreaming in the light, taking control and finding your way. The insights cultivated with the following exercises are designed to offer that light.

JOURNALING

Journaling is critical to success in the world of lucid dreaming. Keeping a journal means you're putting your money where your mouth is and taking your dreams seriously. We'll be using journaling (in the spaces provided throughout the book) in two principal ways: first, for recording your dreams; and second, for working with the exercises in this book. Keep this workbook at your bedside for ready access in recording your dreams. With a little practice you can learn to write in the dark. You can also purchase pens with a soft light directed onto your writing surface. When you click the pen, the light comes on.

I don't usually recommend audio recording your dreams for several reasons. First, you don't want electronic devices by your bed (it's part of the good sleep hygiene we'll discuss later). Second, talking into the device tends to pull you rapidly out of the dream and into waking reality, so you'll forget the dream quickly. Third, even if you whisper, you'll eventually irritate your sleeping partner. But we're all different. If voice recordings work for you, trust that feeling and just do it.

When you're writing down a dream, date the dream and title it. This will help you track your dreams, keep a record of dream themes, help you monitor recurrent dreams, and assist in tracking your progress.

For journaling to work, you have to be honest. Dreams are truth tellers, and being true to your dreams by writing them down accurately is important. This is why many psychologists include dream work in their therapy. Your job is to record the deeper truth that your dreams reveal. Don't edit what you experience.

Your dream journal is also an intimate portrait of your inner landscape. Like any private encounter, your journal is for your eyes only. If you have a sleeping partner or other family members who might see your journal, ask them to respect your privacy. You must feel free to express yourself in the pages ahead; this practice itself can be healing. Worrying about who might see your truth might keep you from expressing it.

EXERCISE: My Lucid Dreaming Aspirations

Think about what you expect from this book, and record it here. What drew you to this book? What do you hope to get from lucid dreaming?

_____

_____

_____

_____

_____

Is there a part of you that's anxious about, intimidated by, or even fearful of lucid dreaming? If so, what generates these feelings? What are your concerns?

_____

_____

_____

_____

By recording a baseline of hopes and fears, expectations and aspirations, you can see how this changes as you go through the book. Whether it's to Vegas, Vanderbilt, or the Vatican, lucid dreaming can take you to dazzling destinations where you can be entertained, educated, or transformed beyond your wildest dreams—or at least within them. Life is short. Time is so precious. By learning how to wake up in your dreams, you can wake up to your life. You can travel to the most exotic inner destinations and bring back a treasure trove of insights to benefit yourself and others. Let's get started.

CHAPTER 1

The Basics

While lucid dreaming may seem new to many people, it's been around for millennia. The term "lucid dreaming" was coined by the Dutch psychiatrist Frederik van Eden (1860–1932). In Western culture, references to lucid dreaming go back as far as Aristotle (350 BCE); in Eastern traditions, lucid dreaming fades into the mist of ancient history. In the Bön tradition of Tibet, lucid dreaming goes back twelve thousand years. The sacred Upanishads (1000 BCE) of Hinduism make frequent allusions to lucid dreaming. Taoism (550 BCE) has a sophisticated lucid dreaming history, and the Buddha, or "Awakened One" (500 BCE), was arguably the ultimate lucid dreamer.

Where did you first hear about lucid dreaming? What was it that piqued your interest?

_____

_____

_____

_____

Lucid dreaming in our modern era took off after it was scientifically proven, first in 1975 by the psychologist Keith Hearne at Hull University in England, and then independently in 1977 by the psychophysiologist Stephen LaBerge at Stanford University. In recent years, lucid dreaming has gradually developed more scientific traction, and popular books have exploded onto the market.

Over 50 percent of people will have at least one lucid dream during their life. Lucid dreaming occurs as early as three years of age, seems to be more natural for children, and then tapers off in the later teens.

WHAT IS A LUCID DREAM?

Having a clear definition of lucid dreaming will help you start to have these dreams. While "lucid" is the most commonly used term for being aware in your dreams, "lucid" is just a term for awareness and its many synonyms. A lucid dream is an aware dream; you're aware of the fact that you're dreaming when you're dreaming. "Conscious dreaming" is another synonym. Lucid dreams can also be called "mindful dreams"; or "recognized dreams"—you're mindful of the fact that you're dreaming, recognizing that you're dreaming while you're dreaming. A lucid dream is also a "non-distracted" dream. You're not lost in the dream or distracted by its contents. Some scientists prefer the term "cognizant dream." Finally, lucid dreams can be called "attentive dreams." You're paying attention to what's really happening, attentive to the fact that you're dreaming.

By contrast, our normal non-lucid dreams are unaware or unconscious dreams. They're mindless dreams, distracted dreams, unrecognized dreams, or inattentive dreams. These synonyms and antonyms are important because they hint at why we have so many non-lucid dreams, and at what we can do to induce lucidity. In other words, they suggest that *lucidity is something we can practice.* We can strengthen our powers of recognition with simple exercises. We can practice mindfulness. We can work with non-distraction. We can become more attentive. We can engage in meditations that develop awareness and increase consciousness. By doing so, we'll naturally find ourselves having lucid dreams.

We can conjure up some magic to have lucid dreams, but the technique is mostly mechanics: simple cause and effect. In Eastern terms, causality is referred to as karma. We're always working with karma, or cause and effect. Another colloquial translation for karma is "habit." What we'll do in the following pages is harness the force of causality and habit to work in our favor. We'll reveal the bad habits that unwittingly bring about non-lucidity, and we'll replace them with good habits that induce lucidity. Having lucid dreams is a natural consequence of this "reveal and replace" strategy.

Always Practicing

The synonyms and antonyms for lucid dreaming are also important because they lead to a startling and humbling discovery: whether we know it or not, we're always practicing. We're always engaging in lucid or non-lucid activity, aware or unaware of what we're doing, mindful or mindless in our lives. If we're not consciously practicing lucidity, our habitual default state is the practice of non-lucidity. It's no wonder we have so many non-lucid dreams!

In other words, we're always meditating. The Tibetan word for "meditation" is *gom*, which means "to become familiar with." We're always becoming more and more familiar with either mindfulness or mindlessness, non-distraction or distraction, lucidity or non-lucidity. Until we consciously engage in mindfulness, non-distraction, and lucidity, we unconsciously default into mindlessness, distraction, and non-lucidity. That's just our habit. So in a very real sense, we've been trained into non-lucidity and continue to practice it every day. This may be why the natural lucid dreams of childhood fade as we become increasingly distracted with the busyness of adolescent and adult life.

EXERCISE: A Look Within

Set this book aside, take a few deep breaths, and look at your mind for the next few minutes. Don't meditate, don't change anything, don't judge or comment on what you see. Just look. Then journal what you see:

_____

_____

_____

_____

If you're honest with yourself, you'll probably see what most of us see: an endless stream of thoughts, images, emotions, or other mental activity. One thought tailgates the next, a bumper-to-bumper traffic jam of thoughts that is the normal rush hour of the modern mind.

Now look at an object in front of you for a few minutes. It can be anything. How long does your mind stay on that object before it drifts into thought or fantasy? Is it a few seconds? Thirty seconds or more? A minute or more?

_____

If you drift away from the object within a few seconds, don't worry; most of us do. That's the fruit of all our mindless practice. We're really good at distraction, or non-lucidity, because we practice it all the time. The good news is that simply noticing this fact is already the practice of lucidity. You're becoming aware of something you were previously not aware of. That's what we're going to be doing with our dreams: becoming aware of, or lucid to, dreams we were previously not aware of.

The Spectrum of Lucidity

Lucid dreaming is not an all-or-nothing affair. You can have a dream where you're barely lucid, which often happens when you're dipping in and out of sleep, or when you wake yourself up from a nightmare. Something suddenly alerts you: Wait a minute, this is just a bad dream, I can wake up from it! At the other end of the spectrum are hyperlucid dreams, when the dream feels more real than waking reality.

Have you already had glimpses of lucidity in your dreams? How about really clear or long non-lucid dreams? Note the dreams that really affected you, or invited a deeper exploration into the world of dreaming altogether.

_____

_____

_____

_____

Dream Length

You can also have short lucid "dreamlets"; these last just a few seconds and often occur as you're falling asleep. These dreamlets are readily accessible ways to explore lucidity. You're probably already having them and just don't know it. Write down your level of experience with these dreamlets. If you haven't had any, write that down. This will help create a baseline record of your dream world.

_____

_____

At the other end of this spectrum are lucid dreams that last over an hour. This is when you can really accomplish things in the dream world. I've had musicians in my seminars tell me that they've performed entire songs in their lucid dreams. Even if it's a non-lucid dream, have you had dreams that seem to last a long time? If you had to guess, what's the longest dream, lucid or non-lucid, that you've had?

_____

_____

Dream Intensity

Hyperlucid dreams that last an hour are game changers. You need to experience just one of these special dreams to change your life. I've never had a near-death experience (NDE), but I suspect that the impact of a NDE is akin to that of these monumental dreams. I've been blessed to have a number of them, and I wake up from each one feeling transformed. We often talk about how "waking up on the wrong side of the bed" can negatively affect our day. Extended hyperlucid dreams are about waking up on the *right* side of the bed, and they can positively affect our entire life.

Think back: have you ever had a dream that impacted your entire day, either positively or negatively? How often does that happen for you? How about a dream that's touched your entire life?

_____

_____

_____

_____

Dream Memory

It's also possible to have a lucid dream and not remember it, or to remember it days later. (This is the difference between what philosophers call "phenomenal consciousness" versus "access consciousness." You can be subliminally conscious of something without being able to report it.) After I mentioned this in a seminar, a student came up to me afterward and said it was an "Aha!" moment. She had been trying to understand why she was getting mysteriously better at a daytime task, one that she was rarely practicing during the day. My comment triggered the memory that she was indeed practicing this task in her dreams—and reaping the fruits in her daily life.

EXERCISE: Entering Dreamland

We usually flop into bed non-lucidly, completely uninterested in and therefore unaware of how the mind transitions from waking to sleeping. *Lucid sleep onset* is about going to sleep more mindfully. To work with lucid sleep onset, which begins the minute you hit the pillow, start to be more curious about how you fall asleep. Pay attention to the transition, and you will start to see things you've never seen before. This paying attention will be your first daytime practice of lucidity. The next time you fall asleep, journal what you experience in the space provided. Be sure to date these entries. Once again, this will serve to establish a baseline "dream graph."

Do you just collapse into sleep? _____

Do thoughts and worries seem to increase when you lie down? _____

Do you observe any gaps between your thoughts as you start to doze off?

_____

What do you notice as you fall asleep? Even if you notice nothing, make a note of that.

_____

_____

_____

Bidirectionality Revisited

Lucid dreaming is an opportunity for the conscious mind to interface with the unconscious mind directly. A key to the practice of lucid dreaming is to use the day to prepare for the night. The essence of the daytime or *diurnal* exercises in the pages ahead is to positively affect your *nocturnal* experience.

What you do during the day is already affecting how you sleep and dream. If you go to sleep all stressed out, you'll tend to have stressful dreams. Write here how your day affects how you sleep and dream:

_____

_____

_____

_____

Conversely, if you spend your day in a peaceful state of mind you'll tend to have peaceful dreams. Have you noticed this in your life?

_____

With the exercises in this book, you're revealing a process that's already operating in your life, then tweaking it. It's another instance of the "reveal and replace" strategy. We're going to install a bunch of "pop-ups" during the day that will ping into your dreams at night, clueing you in to the fact that you're dreaming.

In other words, we're going to use conscious daily practices to hack into a previously restricted domain—the unconscious dreaming mind. It works like this: you'll be going along with a non-lucid dream one night when suddenly something will pop up in the dream and remind you that you'd planted it in your mind during the day: *Hey, this is a dream!* You're instantly lucid.

But in the spirit of bidirectionality, we can use what happens in the night to also transform the day. Lucid dreaming therefore leads to lucid living. With lucid dreaming we're opening a *two-way* street between day and night, which means we can use the insights from our dreams to hack into our conscious minds. It works like this: you'll be going along with the normal flow of your life when suddenly something from your dreams will pop into your mind, perhaps delivering a new insight or inspiration. In my experience, it often happens just when I need it. I might be in a tough discussion with a colleague when a realization from a lucid dream will ping into my mind and remind me to lighten up, that I don't have to take things so seriously. Or I might be in a funk, and an affirming conversation I had in a lucid dream will pop into my mind and cheer me up. This bidirectionality is the basis for many of the benefits we'll discuss in the following chapters.

Whether you're aware of it or not, by engaging in the exercises in this first chapter, you're already starting to open lines of communication between your waking and dreaming mind. It's a form of stealth help. There's more going on here than meets the eye.

By opening these lines of communication, you're replacing a vicious cycle or feedback loop with a virtuous one, inviting insights to flow back and forth, supporting both states. You're cross-pollinating and harvesting from both states of consciousness.

QUESTIONS AND ANSWERS

Can anybody learn how to have lucid dreams?

Yes. Anybody who dreams can "wake up" in their dreams. We have five or six dream periods every night, and *any* dream can become a lucid dream. So the opportunities are there! With some determination, patience, and humor, and given the methods presented in this book, anybody can do it.

Are certain people better at lucid dreaming?

As with any other discipline, it seems that way. Studies have shown that those with better spatial orientation (that is, those better able to adapt their body orientation and posture vis-à-vis their surrounding environment) do better at lucid dreaming. Dream researchers Joe Dane and Robert Van de Castle discovered that people "with a spirit of adventure, who wished to explore the unknown and had a rich curiosity about the ranges of human experiences, were excellent candidates for lucidity."[1]

Are there any contraindications to lucid dreaming, or people who should not do it?

In general, lucid dreams are totally safe, because in essence your mind is totally safe. But anything can be abused, even something inherently healthy. Breathing clean air is healthy—unless we hyperventilate. Drinking clean, safe water is healthy—unless we hyperhydrate. Lucid dreaming can be abused. If someone has escapist or dissociative tendencies, lucid dreaming could worsen those tendencies. If you're emotionally or mentally unstable, or under the care of a mental health professional, check with them before engaging in lucid dreaming. I have taught lucid dreaming to thousands of people and have never experienced anyone developing problems with this practice. Check your motivation, use common sense, and don't be shy about asking a professional for advice if you have any concerns. And trust your intuition. If it doesn't feel right for you, don't do it.

I'm afraid of interrupting my precious sleep. Does lucid dreaming interfere with rest?

Not if you do it properly. We dream the most in the hour or so just before waking up in the morning, after we've already gone through deep restorative sleep. People generally find lucid dreaming to be energizing, not exhausting. I'm often exhilarated and refreshed after my lucid dreams; they actually perk me up. While there are some techniques, like the wake-and-back-to-bed method, that do interrupt normal sleep routines, you can do these on weekends or whenever you have the luxury of sleeping in.

What happens to a person during lucid dreaming?

From the perspective of someone outside, nothing is happening. The sleeper is just dreaming. From the perspective of the dreamer, anything can happen. That's what makes lucid dreaming so exciting. Depending on the clarity, stability, and duration of the dream, you can do virtually anything. The sky isn't even the limit. In a lucid dream, you can soar to the ends of the universe. Mind becomes reality in a lucid dream (what else is a dream made of?), so whatever your mind can conjure up becomes what happens for you. We'll explore what most lucid dreamers tend to do and what meditations like dream yoga invite you to do. It's breathtaking.

Where does dream interpretation fit into lucid dreaming?

Lucid dreaming has a specific bandwidth when it comes to working with dreams. It's explicitly about becoming conscious within a dream. While dream interpretation is valuable and highly recommended (I work with it regularly), lucid dreaming is not really concerned about dream content. It's like meditation, which similarly is not concerned with what arises in your mind when you meditate. Meditation deals with how to change your relationship to what arises. Working with approaches like dream interpretation can help you honor your dreams more, and that can help create an attitude toward dreams that benefits lucid dreaming in a general sense. Working with dream interpretation can also help you with remembering dreams, being more sensitive to the dream world, and opening yourself to the power of dreaming. But lucid dreaming and dream interpretation are two different things.

What kinds of people are interested in lucid dreaming?

In my seminars around the world, and from ample feedback on social media and the internet, I've heard from a tremendous variety of people, with wide-ranging interests. Here are some generalizations: millennials and Gen-X'ers are often drawn to the hip nature of lucid dreaming; they may see it as a sophisticated mental video game. Some boomers like the entertainment value; many others are fascinated by the learning potential. Seniors tend to be captivated by the possibilities of psychological development, and more and more are interested in the spiritual potential. New Agers also love the spiritual aspect—many are interested in how lucid dreaming can help with death. Sometimes a business person or an academic, someone wanting to get a competitive edge, shows up. Many students of the mind—psychologists, psychiatrists, neuroscientists, even the occasional philosopher or shaman—develop an interest. Other people are curious about the latest fads and want to be the first one on their block doing it. More meditators and yoga practitioners are getting into lucid dreaming. Virtually everybody interested in lucid dreaming is a lifelong learner: inquisitive, intrepid, determined, and open-minded. And once someone learns about the mind-bending benefits, they get really interested.

CHAPTER 2

General Benefits

One of the most common questions about lucid dreaming is "Why bother? Life is already so busy; what's in it for me?" Does this describe you? Or are you already sold?

After forty years of exploring these special dreams, I find that the scope and depth of their potential still continue to astound me. The benefits I'll share in the next two chapters may seem almost too good to be true. But the vast literature supports these claims, thousands of students I've worked with continue to verify them, and my own experience confirms these remarkable gains.

Lucid dreaming is subtle. But subtle doesn't mean ineffectual. Thoughts and emotions are very subtle, but they dictate most of our waking lives (called "gross lives" in the Eastern traditions). Virtually everything we say or do starts with a subtle mental impulse. An understated object can control our life's direction, much as the small rudder on a huge ocean liner can control the direction of a massive ship. Lucid dreams have that same power. One dream can change the course of an entire life.

In chaos theory, the *butterfly effect* or, to use the chaos theory term, "sensitive dependence on initial conditions," refers to how a tiny change in one place can result in colossal changes in another place. The image is that of a butterfly flapping its wings in the Bahamas, and the tiny puff from that turbulence eventually building into a cyclone. Lucid dreams work in the same way: you never know how big an effect your nightly dreams can have on your daily life.

In this chapter and the next you will discover the cascade of benefits. From the profane to the profound, from the superficial to the supernatural, the effects of lucid dreaming offer something for everyone.

EXERCISE: Dreams in My Life

Take a few minutes to think back over the role dreams have played in your life so far. What have your dreams offered you? Have you already had some dreams that illuminated aspects of your life? Or helped you solve a problem? Or pointed you in a new direction? List some of your most influential dreams.

_____

_____

_____

_____

_____

If you've had some lucid dreams, how have they changed you?

_____

_____

Reflecting on the importance of dreams—listening to them, honoring them, journaling about them, and sharing them—all serve to establish a conversation between the waking and the dreaming mind. You have a ready conversationalist, even a wise advisor, waiting for you in the silence of the night. You need only to listen to and respect what this deeper part of you has to offer. The best messages and deepest secrets are often whispered.

WHY ARE LUCID DREAMS SO POWERFUL?

Any psychologist will tell you that our conscious lives are dictated by unconscious processes. Backstage always runs what happens onstage. What you do "down there" has vast surface repercussions "up here" in your conscious life. It's akin to the transformative power of hypnosis, but with one big difference: only 5 to 10 percent of the population is highly hypnotizable, whereas virtually everybody dreams and can therefore practice lucid dreaming.

Lucid dreams work with the "tectonic plates" of your experience. When those plates shift beneath you, the shock waves can have deeply moving effects. This is more good news. It means you don't have to have lucid dreams constantly to be changed by them.

In the wisdom traditions, the subtle or unconscious realms give birth to conscious or gross states. In Hinduism, sleeping consciousness, which is even more subtle than dreaming consciousness, is called "causal consciousness." It's the foundation of all coarser states. These subtle but foundational dimensions are the targets for lucid dreaming, and they help us understand why these extraordinary dreams are so transformative.

GENERAL BENEFITS

Before we explore the specific benefits of lucid dreaming in the next chapter, let's take a look at some general ones. The benefits in this chapter are some of the *collateral benefits*, perks that are not part of the lucid dreaming curriculum per se, but healthy side effects. By the time you finish this book, you will see that lucid dreaming is about so much more than just waking up in your dreams. It's about waking up to your life.

In a broad sense, lucid dreaming can feel like stepping out of a bright room and into the dark night. At first you can't see a thing. But if you simply keep your eyes open and remain patient, you will accommodate to the darkness and start to see things that were always there but previously hidden. When you first step into the world of lucid dreaming, you may not see very much. It's initially dark inside. But if you're patient and keep your inner eyes open, all kinds of fascinating things will start to appear.

EXERCISE: Getting to Know Your Dreams

In the space provided, write down what you've first noticed about your dreams since you started reading this book. Are things starting to change? Are you already establishing a new relationship to your dreams?

_____

_____

_____

_____

We're all different and proceed in our own individual ways, but the pattern of progression is something like this: you'll start to see and remember more dreams, your dreams will become clearer, they will last longer, they will become more stable, and you will start to have more impactful dreams. This can all happen *before* you start having lucid dreams, or in conjunction with their occurrence. Does this describe any of your experience?

_____

_____

Because you're starting to relate to your sleeping mind in a more refined way, a host of practical benefits are common. For example, the nocturnal practices can help you transform insomnia. Many participants in my programs struggle with this widespread condition, but because they have learned to better understand sleep cycles (discussed in chapter 4), and have methods to work with their mind during the night (explored in chapters 8 and 9), they have transformed this obstacle into an opportunity.

EXERCISE: Elusive Sleep

Do you struggle with insomnia? If so, have you tried relating to your sleepless mind in a meditative way—and has this approach worked?

_____

_____

Many people suffer from jet lag. While the following methods may not get rid of jet lag, they can help you relate to it differently—to view it as an opportunity to explore the hypnagogic state (the state between wakefulness and sleep) and the hypnopompic state (the transition from sleep to wakefulness) more intensively. Hypnos is the Greek god of sleep, and *gogic* means "heading toward." *Pompic* heads the other way, away from the god of sleep.

If you wrestle with jet lag, have you explored your dreaming mind as you transition into different time zones? If so, what have you learned?

_____

_____

_____

Most people discover that lucid dreaming helps them sleep better, through (1) the good sleep hygiene that we implement with lucid dreaming, (2) the meditations that support lucid dreaming and calm the mind like a nightly pacifier, and (3) removing all fear of the dark and ridding yourself of any anxiety about the unconscious mind and the dreams that bubble up from it.

Some people express a general fear of the dark, which is often a fear of the unknown. We tend to associate light with goodness and dark with evil. "Darkness" is a code word for ignorance and a convenient place to throw a lot of unwanted experiences. This is actually not fair to darkness, which is neutral. But into this black pit we innocently toss many of our personal demons. I've often wondered if this is why children fear there are monsters lurking under the bed. Even some adults feel uneasy about leaving an arm or a leg hanging off the edge of their mattress. Below the bed of the mind is the darkness of the unconscious mind, where all sorts of unwanted phenomena reside.

It could be that this is what you fear lurking down there—your deeper self. The next exercise will help you explore this.

EXERCISE: Hello Darkness

Are you afraid of the dark? If so, why? If not, why not?

_____

_____

_____

What does darkness mean to you? Does it represent anything in particular?

_____

_____

If you have an aversion to darkness, how much do you actually know about what you're avoiding?

_____

_____

_____

Contemplate your relationship to darkness. For many people, darkness is an unconscious landfill. "Out of sight, out of mind" applies to how some of us treat darkness, filling it with many of the rejected aspects of our experience. We then fear darkness because it represents what we don't want to see. It becomes the refuse heap of our refused experience. Outer and inner darkness is where we try to hide our innermost fears. Our ease or anxiety with outer darkness is a reliable indicator for how we feel about the inner kind. "Out of sight, out of mind" may mean "out of sight and into the unconscious mind," which is where dreams take place, and why some people fear their dreams. Lucid dreaming turns on the night-light and can help you see all this, freeing you from inner fears and even transforming your relationship to outer darkness.

Lucid dreaming can show you the relationship of outer and inner darkness and make you feel safe exploring both, because *lucid dreaming is a practice of light*. "Light" is a code word for awareness ("let there be light!"), and what doesn't improve with more awareness?

As part of my spiritual training, I engage in traditional dark retreats. I'll enter a pitch-black cabin to remove all distractions and to look deeply within. These cabins are specifically constructed to remove any light pollution. It's like the observatories that scientists build on secluded mountaintops, away from any distracting light source. When things get really dark, astronomers can peer into the edges of the distant universe and see things never seen before.

It's beyond the scope of this book to explore dark retreat, but one aspect applies here. Every time I go into my dark cabin, it takes a few days to caulk up the tiniest leaks of light. I'm always struck by how powerful light is, and how the most miniscule pinhole can illuminate so much space. The effect is much greater than the cause. Light has an extraordinary ability to leak in and spread everywhere.

In a similar way, the inner light from our lucid dreams can illuminate so much more than our dreams. This is yet another reason we don't need to have lucid dreams all the time to be enlightened by them. A tiny pinhole of inner light can illuminate vast inner space.

These are just a few of the general benefits of lucid dreaming. I'm certain you can add to this list. In the space provided, write down the benefits you discover as you go through this book.

_____

_____

_____

_____

_____

QUESTIONS AND ANSWERS

If lucid dreaming can tap into these deeper dimensions, like causal consciousness, it sounds like it can help me discover who I really am, right?

Absolutely. But only if you want to go this deep. Many people prefer to stay on the surface of lucid dreaming, and that's fine. There is plenty to do at these outer levels, and a host of benefits. But for those intrepid explorers looking for a deeper dive, lucid dreaming—and especially its evolution into dream yoga—can indeed take you to the center of yourself. There are many ways to explore the darkness of the night and the darkness of the unconscious mind via lucid dreaming. I'll show you the possibilities, point out the directions, give you some tips on how to get there, and then send you out—or in this case "in"—on your own.

Is fear of the dark, of the unknown, the only thing people are afraid of when it comes to lucid dreaming?

First of all, most people are not afraid. Most people are excited about the possibilities. But this is a great question, because it can lead to some deep reflections and discoveries. While some people *are* afraid of the dark, others are actually afraid of the light—of being too awake and aware. Marianne Williamson observed, "Our deepest fear is not that we are inadequate. Our deepest fear is that we are powerful beyond measure. It is our light, not our darkness, that most frightens us."[2]

There is tremendous power in the darkness of the night and the deepest recesses of the unconscious mind. We can tap into that power when we bring it into the light of consciousness with these practices of lucidity. But some people prefer to sleep, in the spiritual sense. Instead of putting their head in the proverbial sand, they put it under the covers. They just don't want to know. They prefer to stay distracted with daytime external activities, lost in non-lucidity. That's okay. This is not meant as a judgment. But it shows that even talking about lucidity is revelatory. With these nocturnal practices, you can start to see things about yourself you've never seen, even before you hit the sack. Most people reading this book are probably tired of "oversleeping" and have an interest in "waking up." And when they do, they can inspire others to do the same. Williamson also said, "As we let our own light [lucidity] shine, we unconsciously give other people permission to do the same."[3]

So some people are afraid of awareness, of becoming lucid?

Awareness is power, but some people have not yet realized this. Until they do, they remain disempowered, allowing others to control their lives. They don't realize they could take control, so they spend their waking lives as if in a non-lucid dream. On an even deeper level, many people unconsciously submit to the power of their unconscious mind and hand their lives over to deeply ingrained habits, sleepwalking through their "conscious" lives. This is the sleep that the buddhas ("the awakened ones") wake up from.

CHAPTER 3

Mental, Physical, and Spiritual Benefits

The entertainment value (or "Vegas" part) of lucid dreaming is worth the dedicated effort that is the price of admission. Lucid dreaming is better than going to an IMAX theater, more fun than a 3D Cinemax, more captivating than virtual reality. Some lucid dreaming aficionados look down on this and hardly consider it a benefit. But entertainment has its place. Do you need a brief vacation on the beach but just can't afford it? Lucid dreaming provides the ticket. If you are affected by a disability, you can be free of it in a lucid dream. Paraplegics can run and dance, the blind can see, and the hearing-impaired can enjoy music again. Lucid dreaming can be a form of time travel: the old can return to their youth. If you're imprisoned or confined in any way, a lucid dream can set you free. You can transcend any physical limitation in your dreams.

The haunting documentary *Unrest* chronicles the devastating effects of myalgic encephalomyelitis, or ME, a condition better known as chronic fatigue syndrome, or CFS. The film depicts a woman confined to bed rest virtually 24/7 for many years. Even sitting up in bed caused overwhelming fatigue. She remarked that the only way she could endure her extreme confines was by escaping into her mind. Such a patient could be a prime candidate for the benefits of lucid dreaming.

The shadow side of entertainment and escape is, of course, escapism. But I don't know a single lucid dream junkie in this negative sense. Most of the dreamers I know enjoy the freedom of these magical dreams, but also appreciate the higher opportunities.

When you first heard about lucid dreaming, how much of this entertainment aspect appealed to you? Is this one of the main reasons you're interested in lucid dreaming?

_____

_____

_____

REHEARSAL

Lucid dreams are frequently used to rehearse things, like a presentation or performance, so you can use them to develop proficiency, increase confidence, and reduce anxiety. Anything you can do in life you can do in a lucid dream. As a pianist, I have practiced entire piano pieces in my lucid dreams and rehearsed talks. I'll enter the practice room or auditorium of my dreams and go to work. A YouTube clip about a gifted German lucid dreamer reveals the legitimacy of this claim (http://www.dw.com/en/improve-skills-in-dreams/av-38247611). The dreamer refines his swimming skills, and his ability to play the ukulele, by rehearsing these tasks in his dreams.

The great pianist Arthur Rubinstein could mentally practice a composition and then perform it without further physical rehearsal. He learned the piece purely in his mind without ever touching the piano. Skiers will often be seen before a competition racing through the gates in their mind, weaving their heads back and forth in a mental simulation of the course. Research has shown that the virtual reality of a dream is more effective than the conscious, directed imagination in creating neural connections in the absence of actual physical movement.

If you don't have enough hours in the day to fine-tune your golf swing, practice your guitar, or prepare for that presentation, you can add a "night shift" to your life by becoming lucid in your dreams. Is there something you want to get better at? Write it down and *make the aspiration* to become lucid in your dreams so you can practice this activity:

"I want to become lucid so that I can become better at _____

_____ ''

CONFLICT RESOLUTION

If you're in counseling or therapy and working to resolve an interpersonal issue, the person you're having the problem with doesn't have to be there physically for you to resolve the issue. They need only be there phenomenally, in your mind. You can work out the problem with your therapist by engaging in role-play, creating imaginary scenarios, or using a host of other proven methods, none of which involve the physical presence of the problematic person. In a lucid dream, the person you're having some difficulty with isn't in your dream physically, but they do appear to you. That's enough, because the physical body of the person is rarely the problem. The problem is how we relate to that body or to that person. And relationship tangles can be cleared up in a lucid dream.

People use lucid dreams in this therapeutic way, working out issues just as effectively as the therapy they've engaged with in daily life. As in real-life therapy, this level of dream work is not always easy or pleasant, but it can be just as successful. If you're working with a therapist trained in traditional dream work, lucid dream therapy can be a viable supplement.

Researchers at the Max Planck Institutes discovered that the anterior prefrontal cortex, the part of the brain involved in self-reflection, is significantly larger in frequent lucid dreamers. This suggests that lucid dreamers are exercising a level of awareness that can be measured, an awareness that is at the heart of many of these benefits.

Are you struggling with an interpersonal issue? If so, make the aspiration that you want to resolve this issue in your dreams. Be specific in writing down what you want to clean up.

_____

_____

_____

_____

Sometimes this aspiration will come to fruition in a non-lucid dream, delivering insights into how you could work with a situation. At other times, your intention to resolve this issue in your dreams will trigger a lucid dream, which is even more fruitful.

WORKING WITH GRIEF

In a similar vein, you can clear up unfinished interpersonal issues with others, even those who have died. Death is the end of a body, but it's not the end of a relationship. It's common to have dreams about people who have died, recently or even long before, especially if they were close to you. As we'll see in chapter 6, becoming sensitized to the presence of a deceased person in your dreams is a potent way to induce lucidity by working with *dreamsigns*—things that can occur only in the context of your dreams and can clue you in to the fact that you're dreaming. For example, if your dead father appears to you, alive and functioning, you are dreaming. You can use his presence as a sign that you must be dreaming, so you become lucid. If you had some unresolved issues with your father, you can work through them in your lucid dreams, using the same tenets as for conflict resolution.

As challenging as it may initially be, you can also have lucid dreams about an impending death of a loved one, feel that sense of loss, and use this form of anticipatory grief to help you process the real grief. These dreams can also help you realize that you can't take anybody for granted and therefore take steps to invigorate a relationship with a living loved one. Contemplating impermanence is a poignant irony: frame something with the truth of transience, and it brings it more fully into life. This is one reason why rainbows and flowers are so special: they just don't last. You appreciate things more when you know that those things don't endure.

Have you had dreams about deceased family or friends? Do these dreams make you feel better, or worse? Give it some thought and record your response here.

_____

Make the aspiration that the next time you see a deceased loved one in your dream, you will become lucid and engage that loved one in conversation. Even if it doesn't work at first, you're starting to plant seeds for future dreams. How does this possible encounter make you feel?

_____

_____

_____

_____

If it doesn't feel right for you, release the aspiration and any efforts to bring it about.

PROBLEM SOLVING

Lucid dreaming has been shown to significantly improve problem solving. Problems often remain unsolved because we're too involved with them, too close to the issue. It's like trying to see the inside of your eyelids; you can't see them because you're too close. Intense, all-encompassing involvement is precisely what defines a non-lucid dream. We're too involved with the dream to realize it's just a dream. Lucidity allows us to step back and see things not seen before. This new perspective transforms a non-lucid dream into a lucid one, and the quality of perspective can continue in waking life. It can help us see things that others don't see, or that we didn't previously see.

One study states, "For the insight that leads to lucidity, people also seem to step back from the obvious interpretation and consider a remote and, at the time, implausible option—that it is all a dream."[4] The dream researcher Clare Johnson writes, "Lucid dream creativity likely does not stop when we wake up, but leaves its traces in our waking brain, thereby enhancing our everyday problem solving skills, artistic courage, and creative thought processes."[5]

Have you ever asked your dreams for help with a problem? Was any insight delivered in your dreams? Write down the problem you most want help with, and see if by the end of the book some insight comes to you in your non-lucid or lucid dreams.

———————————————————————————————————————

———————————————————————————————————————

———————————————————————————————————————

———————————————————————————————————————

———————————————————————————————————————

CREATIVITY

Lucid dreaming is the ultimate simulator. Artists, writers, musicians, and innovators are increasingly using lucid dreaming as a way to enhance their arts and crafts. Whatever you can imagine, you can create in the virtual reality of your dreams. Einstein came up with many of his revolutionary insights by performing "thought experiments," visualizing what it might be like to race alongside a photon, for example. "Dream experiments" have even more potential, because the simulation is enhanced.

On a general level, creative impulses often arise from the unconscious mind, which is like an untapped natural resource. In a lucid dream, you're face-to-face with the unconscious mind and can therefore tap into its creative potential more directly. Salvador Dalí and Thomas Edison devised similar methods to farm the interface between the dreaming and waking mind. Reclined in a comfortable chair (or some variation of the following), they would hold a key in one hand, suspended above a plate. As they dozed off, the key would drop onto the plate, waking them up. Dalí would then sketch any insights from this brief dip, then repeat the technique. Edison would jot down his innovative ideas. These creative masters captured the richness of their unconscious mind as it burst into conscious awareness.

The literature is replete with insights and breakthroughs coming from the dream state. When presented with a problem, we don't say, "Let me drink on it," or "I need to exercise on that one." We say, "Let me sleep on it." Lucid dreaming makes you a better listener, more sensitive to your dreaming mind, and therefore more likely to tune in to the bed of creativity. The psychoanalyst Janine

Chasseguet-Smirgel writes, "The process of creation [is] accompanied by the capacity to communicate with the most primitive layers of the unconscious."[6] And Clare Johnson adds, "If this capacity to communicate includes the ability to ask the unconscious—in the form of the dreaming mind—directly for creative inspiration, then the lucid dreamer could well have an advantage over the non-lucid dreamer."[7]

Both Freud and Jung credit dreams for some of their most seminal ideas. We see it in examples from Paul McCartney's *Yesterday*, to the discovery of the structure of the benzene molecule, to Mary Shelley's *Frankenstein*; creative impulses await anyone in the silence of the night. (For a rich offering of these anecdotes, see Deirdre Barrett's 2001 *The Committee of Sleep: How Artists, Scientists, and Athletes Use Dreams for Creative Problem-Solving—and How You Can Too*.) Many of these insights happened spontaneously, without direct incubation or effort. But with direct incubation, the creativity latent in the dream world is boundless.

Have you had creative insights come to you during the night? Not just in your dreams, but even those dreamy states before or after dreaming? If so, write down a few instances when an "Aha!" moment came to you during the night.

_____

_____

_____

_____

_____

CRUX OF THE BENEFITS

One remarkable fact about lucid dreaming, and the core of many of its benefits, is that the physiological effects (in terms of neuronal connections) on your brain and your body of the actions you perform in a lucid dream are virtually identical to the neurological effects of doing these actions in real life. *Dreaming of doing something is neurologically equivalent to actually doing it!* Practicing the piano in your dreams can actually make you a better pianist.

If you're working out a logical problem in your dream, the left hemisphere of your brain is activated, just as it would be in daily life. If you play the piano in a lucid dream, your right hemisphere is activated, just as in real life. Your brain can't seem to tell the difference between something real or dreamt.

A revolutionary insight in neuroscience was the discovery that the brain is highly malleable or "plastic"—a quality termed *neuroplasticity*. What you do with your mind actually changes your brain. As Clare Johnson explains, "The imagination can form the brain almost to the same degree as actual experience."[8] So by dreaming about something, you can literally change your brain (what scientists call *downward causation*). Dream activities are not stuck in the dream world. They download into your brain, which can further download into your life. Think about that. Or better yet, dream about it.

Body Benefits

It's not just your brain that can change with lucid dreaming. You can actually improve the performance of your body. What you do with your dream body has an effect on your physical body. Many people have a physical orgasm when their dream body has an orgasm, or wake up with their physical heart pounding when their dream heart was pounding from a nightmare. Dream researcher Daniel Erlacher says, "In one experiment we asked participants to dream about doing deep knee bends. Even though their bodies weren't moving, their heart and respiration rates increased slightly as if they were exercising."[9]

A study in the *Journal of Sports Science* suggests that lucid dreaming can be used to help athletes improve their performance. Lucid dreaming researcher Kelly Bulkeley offers four remarkable implications for lucid dreaming:

- It could provide a safe arena in which high-performance athletes can practice dangerous moves and risky routines, developing skills at the furthest edges of their abilities.

- It could provide injured athletes with an opportunity to continue training and skill-building during their rehabilitation.

- It could enable underprivileged athletes to engage in effective practice of their sports even if they have limited access to physical facilities.

- It could give athletes at all levels a powerful psychological means of focusing their minds for optimal game-day performance.[10]

Want to get in some extra training or gain an edge on the competition? You don't always have to go back to the gym; you could simply go back to bed.

What physical activity would you like to improve? Even though it may not happen right away, write down your aspirations, and then see if your wishes come true in your dreams—and eventually in your life.

_____

_____

_____

_____

_____

Healing

The connection between the dream body and the physical body offers the potential for lucid dreaming to be used for healing. In the Eastern view, the outer body is an expression of the inner subtle body, which is deeply connected with the dream body (we'll explore this in chapter 9). Eastern medical systems target the subtle body with practices like acupuncture and moxibustion in an effort to heal the gross physical body.

In the West, guided imagery is used to facilitate healing, as in the cancer work of Dr. Carl Simonton. He reports that patients who supplemented standard chemotherapy and radiation treatments with healing imagery survived on average twice as long as expected.[11] Nowhere is imagery more potent, and therefore potentially transformative, than in a dream. In other words, the transformative power of the imagination is proportional to how real it feels, and there's nothing more real in terms of the imagination than a vivid dream. Doctors Dennis Jaffe and David Bresler write, "Mental imagery mobilizes the latent, inner powers of the person, which have immense potential to aid in the healing process and in the promotion of health."[12]

It's too early to say for sure, but preliminary data suggests that you may be able to initiate self-healing by consciously visualizing your dream body as healthy. If you can "heal" your dream body, to what extent will you also heal your physical body? One doctor published a paper about a patient with a twenty-two-year history of chronic pain who cured himself overnight with a single lucid dream. The psychiatrist Mauro Zappaterra says, "I'm no expert on lucid dreaming, but the man woke up with no pain. He said it was like his brain had shut down and rebooted. A few days later, he walks in to the VA pharmacy and actually returns his medication. To me that's pretty convincing evidence."[13]

If you are struggling with any physical disorders or illnesses, note them here:

_____

Pause and visualize that part of your body as completely healed. Now set the intention to do the same thing in your dreams. If you have a lucid dream, see that part of your dream body as healthy and whole. Try to heal yourself from the inside out. The next time you have a lucid dream, when you wake up, write down what you experienced when you visualized your dream body as perfectly healthy and whole.

_____

_____

_____

Resolving Nightmares

Lucid dreaming has been shown to remove or greatly reduce nightmares, which afflict up to 85 percent of the population. In a lucid dream we can reframe the experience and create different endings to recurrent bad dreams. Nightmares often occur when rejected aspects of our being return to us in the form of monstrous dream figures. Instead of running away from the monster—our default reaction in a non-lucid dream, which keeps the monster alive—in a lucid dream we can turn around and face the monster with the confidence born of our lucidity. We can wake up to the fact that it's only our mind, it's only a dream, and we're in control. We do not need to be afraid.

By understanding that these scary aspects are simply calling out for healing, we can reintegrate them back into our being and become whole. If you have recurrent nightmares, this reintegration will cause them to stop. The poet Rainer Maria Rilke wrote, "Perhaps everything that frightens us is, in its deepest essence, something helpless that wants our love."[14] And Stephen LaBerge, the father of Western lucid dreaming, shares this: "When you meet a monster in your lucid dream, sincerely greet him like a long-lost friend, and that is what he will be."[15]

The next time you have a nightmare, of course something will eventually wake you up from it. If it is not sheer terror (which does happen), but a sudden insight, *Hey, this is just a bad dream!*, recognize that as a moment of lucidity. We usually use that moment as an eject button to get us out of the dream. As a practice, try to catch that brief instant of lucidity, and instead of waking up and running away from the dream, stay with it. This skill is a bit more advanced, so don't worry if it doesn't happen at first. Even trying it is revelatory.

Waking up to the fact that it's just a dream, even if it's a scary one, strips the dream of its nightmarish power. "Nightmare practice" is a part of dream yoga, in which a dream yogi will consciously create frightening situations in their lucid dream as a way to work with fear.

EXERCISE: Embracing Your Nightmares

If it feels right for you, try this practice the next time you have a nightmare:

1.   Stay with the bad dream; don't run away.

2.   If something is chasing you, turn around and face it.

3.   If it's a monster, look it in the eye.

4.   If your lucidity is strong, step toward the monster with open arms and embrace it.

In short, do the opposite of what you would normally do.

Now journal your experience, describing any difficulties or revelations. Notice whether even just the thought of putting this into practice gives you a new feeling of power.

_____

_____

_____

_____

In my experience with this exercise, the monster will disappear or dissolve into me. Either way, I wake up with my heart racing not from fear, but from the power I feel of having the courage to face my fears, and from the resulting sense of resolution.

Phobias

If you have an irrational fear—of heights, spiders, public speaking, flying, snakes, or any other phobia—you can work with your anxiety in the safety of your dreams. You can conjure up a dream spider and establish a better relationship with the fear. When a dream yogi is in a fearful dream, they celebrate it as an opportunity to transcend fear. As with nightmares, this level of practice is not for everyone, so don't worry if it doesn't resonate with you. We're all different, and the curriculum of this night school is as varied as that of any university.

All the nocturnal practices are elective. But is fear elective? Are phobias elective? Are unwanted experiences elective? For those wanting to go deeper into the night, lucid dreaming provides an opportunity to work with these shadowy elements.

Describe any phobias here: _____

_____

_____

Then set the intention that the next time you experience any of them in a dream, you will relate to that fearful situation, knowing that it's just a dream. This technique is from the family of *systematic desensitization* therapies, which have been around since the 1950s.

After you do this in a lucid dream, write down what you experienced:

_____

_____

_____

_____

SPIRITUAL BENEFITS

The highest levels of lucid dreaming transition into dream yoga and the practices that lead to spiritual insight. The Buddha practiced dream yoga, and for the 2,600 years since, these nocturnal meditations have been part of this noble tradition. In both Buddhism and Hinduism, of the three principal states of consciousness—waking, sleeping, and dreaming—the coarsest state, the one with the *least* potential for spiritual evolution, is the waking state. Henry David Thoreau said, "Our truest life is when we are in dreams awake." The meditation master Namkhai Norbu Rinpoche says,

> It is easier to develop your practices in a dream than in the daytime. In the daytime we are limited by our material body, but in a dream our function of mind and our consciousness of the senses are unhindered. We can have more clarity. Thus there are more possibilities. . . If a person applies

a practice within a dream, the practice is nine times more effective than when it is applied during the waking hours.[16]

It can also happen quickly, as Clare Johnson notes, "I close my [dream] eyes. All imagery vanishes and it goes black. Instantly I am deeply relaxed, it's so much faster than meditation in the waking state and I marvel at how deep I go within seconds, with no back discomfort or sensory distractions."[17]

In the Eastern view of reality, you can purify karma in a lucid dream and prevent negative karma from coming to fruition in the waking state. Remember that karma is just another word for habit, which means you can clean up bad habits in your dreams. According to Buddhism, karma often starts to ripen in the subtle dream state before it manifests in the gross waking state, which means it can be purified at this more subtle level. The Swiss psychiatrist Carl Jung supported a similar view. Dream yoga expert Alan Wallace says, "Can karma come to maturation in the dream state? Definitely yes. [Dreams] can purify karma, rather than having it come to full maturation in some waking state. Better to get rid of it in the dream state."[18]

In this regard, a sensitive relationship to your dreams can literally save your life, because you're working with the blueprints of your experience before they become fully constructed in manifest reality. Countless stories refer to dreams of premonition, or *prodromal dreams*—dreams that later came true. These dreams often happen just before waking up in the morning, and they carry extra power. They just feel more important. (See the chapter "The Disembodied Woman" in *The Man Who Mistook His Wife for a Hat*, by Oliver Sacks. Or see this haunting video about a recurrent dream that accurately predicts a plane crash: https://vimeo.com/237676110.)

Have you had dreams of premonition? Did any of these dreams actually come true? Do these sorts of "psychic" dreams excite you—or intimidate you?

_____

_____

_____

_____

_____

INCUBATED DREAMS

You can also incubate lucid dreams to receive guidance. The ancient Egyptians practiced this, as did the Chinese, Mesopotamians, Greeks, and many wisdom traditions. The literature is full of accounts of people who asked for, and then received, messages and teachings in their dreams.

Lucid dream incubation is a bit different, because with a lucid dream you can engage in conscious dialogue with the messenger. Tenzin Palmo, a British nun, spent twelve years in solitary retreat in the Himalayas, often snowed in for months in her cave. She said that this was never a problem, because whenever she needed guidance or support she'd ask for it and get it directly from her dreams. When I was on a three-year retreat of my own I did the same thing. Sometimes I'd find myself sitting at the feet of one of my teachers, fully lucid, and ask him questions just as I did in waking reality. Whether these teachers were somehow infiltrating my mind or were merely aspects of my own deeper mind appearing in the form of a teacher doesn't matter. The message is what's important, not the messenger.

Have you ever asked for guidance in your dreams? Did you then receive it? If so, did the information come in a regular dream or was the dream lucid?

_____

_____

_____

_____

You can also incubate dreams for others and become a *surrogate dreamer*. Surrogate dreaming is a common practice in shamanic traditions and frequently employed in Tibetan Buddhism. Meditation masters like the Dalai Lama are frequently asked to help locate the reincarnation of another spiritual master (see the documentary *Unmistaken Child*). The meditation master then sleeps on it, and within a few days has a dream about where to find the reincarnated teacher.

I have never actively incubated dreams for others, but I have received such dreams spontaneously. Some of these dreams were lucid, others were not. When I have had the courage to share these dreams with the people for whom they were intended, the information from the dream was always helpful. I felt like a courier of sorts, delivering messages to their rightful destination. Anybody who believes in the power of dreams or is open to the possibility can engage in surrogate dreaming.

DREAMS TO DIE FOR

Finally, one can use the darkness of the night to prepare for the darkness of death. According to a number of wisdom traditions, sleeping, dreaming, and dying are intimately connected. In Greek mythology, Hypnos (the god of sleep) and Thanatos (the god of death) are not just brothers—they are twins. In Buddhism, dream yoga came about principally as a way to prepare for death. *Bardo yoga* in the Tibetan tradition, which helps one prepare for "the dream at the end of time," works with lucid dreaming extensively. The Tibetans also say that certain dreams may portend illness and death.

When you realize that there is a disembodied (nonphysical) dimension of reality—the dream state, which can be as real as or even more real than your experience of the physical waking state—it suggests that experience might continue without a gross physical body. With lucid dreaming, you can learn to disidentify with, let go of, or "die to" your physical body and learn to identify with a more subtle body. According to many spiritual traditions, this subtle body transcends physical death. The Mexican healer Sergio Magaña writes, "You will know when you have overcome your fear of death when you start lucid dreaming regularly, because that is like dying."[19] In the last year of her life, one woman reported having 160 lucid dreams and said, "These dreams teach me to die."[20]

Have you ever felt that falling asleep is a bit like "resting in peace," or dying? Does this thought spook you? Or does it give you some hope that you could actually use sleep and dreams as a way to prepare for "the dream at the end of time"?

_____

_____

_____

_____

_____

In the curriculum of our night school, these more advanced practices are like graduate school. They're not for everybody. But they do point out the incredible potential of our dreams, and just how far these nocturnal practices can take you.

QUESTIONS AND ANSWERS

Does lucid dreaming interfere with creative impulses? Isn't it better to just let the unconscious mind play out in our dreams, without conscious manipulation?

Lucid dreaming manipulates the dream only if you choose to do so. A *witness lucid dream* is when you're fully lucid in the dream, but elect to just watch. You witness the unfolding of the dream like you're watching a movie, without changing a thing.

While I find all these benefits quite inspiring, part of me also finds them a bit intimidating. I can't even have a lucid dream, let alone do these amazing things in them. Do people really do these things?

Yes, they most certainly do. We all have that capacity. The vast potential of the human mind is largely untapped. At this point, let these remarkable benefits inspire you. As with any other new discipline, it takes some time to master these activities. So be patient, and let things develop in their own way. Even when you do progress in lucid dreaming, it's not like you do every one of the things mentioned in this chapter. You could, but people usually end up playing around with several of these exercises in their lucid dreams and don't tie themselves into knots trying to do everything. A key to success is enjoying what you do, delighting in the small achievements, and marveling at even the briefest moments of lucidity. The rest will unfold in its own time. So relax. Flip through this catalog of possibilities and just enjoy the ride.

If I have a lucid dream, can I meet with someone who has died?

It depends on whom you ask. Traditional dream scholars and most scientist types (neuroscientists, psychologists, and the like) would say no. Shamans, mystics, and indigenous healers would say yes. I would say yes, but I can't do so with absolute certainty. This question is akin to that of receiving teachings in your dreams. Is the teacher somehow infiltrating your dream, or is your inner guru just making an appearance in a form you can relate to? There is value in the power of an open question, one that can't be definitely answered. Keeping an open mind is perhaps the main point with questions like these. I try to tread a middle way between staying open to radical ideas (that's the mystic in me) and maintaining a healthy skepticism (honoring the scientist in me).

CHAPTER 4

The Science

Learning about the science of sleep can help you have lucid dreams because it shows you when to apply the induction methods. There are times to ramp up your efforts during the night and times to just sleep. If you're a meditator, learning about the stages of sleep will also help you understand what's happening when you dip in and out of sleep on your meditation cushion. It can help you practice both lucid sleep onset and how to maintain awareness as you doze off during your meditation or drift into sleep while in bed. Knowing about the stages is like putting up road signs on the highway to lucidity, showing you where you're at in the process of sleep, and when to speed up or slow down.

TYPES OF SLEEP

There are two main kinds of sleep: non-REM and REM. REM stands for the rapid eye movement that sleep scientists observe when a subject is dreaming the most. You can see the eyes darting around under closed lids when people sleep, and if you were to wake someone up at that time they would almost always say they were dreaming. You may have noticed this as you watched someone sleep; if not, take your next opportunity to observe. REM sleep was first described in 1953.

Non-REM sleep is associated with deep relaxation and restoration and is mostly dreamless. When people are woken up in a sleep lab during REM, about 80 percent will report that they were dreaming; if they're woken up during non-REM sleep, 45 percent will report a dream.

Lucid dreaming does not target non-REM sleep, even though lucidity can be attained anytime we're dreaming. We put up a DO NOT DISTURB sign during non-REM sleep and get the restorative sleep we need. This is why lucid dreaming, if done properly, doesn't make us tired. With lucid dreaming, we're also engaging our sleep cycles at a time when the brain is as active as it is during the day, as we'll see.

REM sleep accounts for about 25 percent of our sleep; it's also associated with muscle twitches, an active brain, and muscle atonia, in which the voluntary muscles of the body are temporarily paralyzed as we dream—nature's way of protecting ourselves and others from acting out our dreams. The body becomes like a limp rag doll. This atonia usually goes unrecognized, but we can became aware of it during an out-of-sequence REM state, in which it's called *sleep paralysis*. We're not supposed to be conscious of our body in REM sleep. We're supposed to be sleeping or dreaming. But sometimes the cycles get scrambled.

People often experience sleep paralysis as a panic-inducing inability to move or speak, usually encountered when they're partly awake and partly asleep. If you don't know what's happening, it can be an unsettling experience, as if someone is holding you down or you're constrained in a straitjacket. If you have ever had this experience, what was your reaction to it?

_____

_____

Several studies have found that sleep paralysis is the origin of many alien abduction stories.[21] But if you do know what's happening, sleep paralysis can be a fascinating experience. In rare instances, like REM sleep behavior disorder, this atonia doesn't happen, and people who are sound asleep do things like beat up sleeping partners, or even kill.

Sleepwalking and sleep talking are different; they usually occur in non-REM sleep when there is no atonia.

Now that you know what it is, the next time you experience sleep paralysis, bring your new understanding to it, and observe this *Twilight Zone*–type experience. Instead of freaking out when you can't move or speak, experiment with it. Try moving your arms and see what happens—or doesn't. Be curious, like a good scientist. This approach will dispel the panicky feeling and allow you to explore an altered state of consciousness. When you awaken, write down here how you related to sleep atonia.

_____

_____

_____

_____

Getting enough sleep is important for lucid dreaming, and of course it's critically important for your health. Humans need around an hour of sleep for every two hours they're awake. Yet the average person in developed Western societies sleeps less than seven hours a night, which is about two hours less than a century ago. The World Health Organization now labels lack of sleep as a global health epidemic. Sleep may be more important than food. Animals will die of sleep deprivation before they die of starvation.

How many hours of sleep do you get a night? Do you feel like it's enough? If not, what can you do to get the rest you need?

_____

_____

_____

_____

_____

STAGES OF SLEEP

Every night we go through four stages of sleep in roughly ninety-minute cycles. Each stage is associated with a brain wave frequency, which can be recorded by an EEG (electroencephalograph), that is correlated with brain activity. Waking consciousness is associated with beta and alpha, sleep with theta and delta. Beta waves pulsate at a frequency of 13 to 40 cycles per second, or *hertz*; these are associated with states of concentration and stress. Alpha waves have a frequency of 8 to 13 hertz and are associated with more relaxed waking states. When we go to sleep, the brain downshifts from waking beta and alpha to theta (4 to 8 hertz), and eventually into the "neutral" deep sleep state of delta (0 to 4 hertz). It's as if we transition from the passing lane of our speedy lives to a tranquil rest area.

As we begin to decelerate, we enter the *hypnagogic* phase. (A dream that happens in this phase, or in the wakening hypnopompic phase, is called a *liminal dream*; we'll explore these in chapter 12.) This is when we've pulled off the highway and are coasting along the off-ramp to our rest area. During this early sleep phase, it's common to experience a sensation of falling, someone calling out to you, or other "hypnagogic hallucinations." This sense of falling is often accompanied by an involuntary full-body contraction of the muscles called a myoclonic (or hypnic) jerk. Have you experienced this jerk? Has it startled you into a momentary panic? Write your response here.

_____

_____

Now write about what it's like for you when you dip through the hypnagogic state. Exploring these dips invites a heightened sense of awareness in this phase of presleep, which is a form of lucidity, or lucid sleep onset.

_____

_____

_____

Sleep stages one through three are all classified as non-REM sleep:

Stage One

The first stage lasts five to ten minutes, and amounts to 4 to 5 percent of total sleep. It's still easy to wake someone up in this stage. If you do wake them up, the person often will say they weren't really sleeping. Brain waves during stage one downshift from alpha to theta. Though this presleep state is brief, we can still work with lucid sleep onset and explore hypnagogic states.

Stage Two

This stage can last up to fifty minutes during the night's first sleep cycle. It is characterized by a decrease in breathing, heart rate, and body temperature. The brain is still mostly in theta, but now it's harder to wake the person up. We spend 45 to 55 percent of total sleep here. Stages one and two are considered light sleep.

Stage Three

This combined stage of what used to be stages three and four of deep sleep, marked by delta waves on the EEG, starts 35 to 45 minutes after falling asleep and lasts about thirty minutes in the first ninety-minute sleep cycle. It's hard to wake up someone who's in stage three, and if you do manage to rouse them, they're often disoriented and grumpy, a phenomenon called *sleep inertia*.

Recall a time when you were awakened from this deep sleep stage. Did you find it jarring? Describe the experience:

_____

_____

_____

_____

_____

Stage three is characterized by slow rhythmic breathing and profound relaxation. This is deep restorative sleep, in which the body is fully off-line. This stage performs a lot of maintenance, releasing human growth hormone and making cellular and biological repairs. Michael Perlis, director of the Behavioral Sleep Medicine program at the University of Pennsylvania, says of this stage, "You're talking about a level of brain deactivation that is really rather intense. Stage 3 sleep is not far removed from coma or brain death."[22] For people with sleep apnea (a sleep disorder second only to insomnia in prevalence), this is the stage of sleep that is continually interrupted, and that's a major reason sleep apnea is so damaging.

The time we spend in delta sleep decreases as we age, from about 20 percent for young adults to 3 percent by midlife. By age sixty-five, this slow-wave sleep can virtually disappear. Because the release of growth hormone also decreases, lack of deep sleep can account for many aspects of aging, including increased body fat, loss of muscle tone and strength, thinning of the skin, diminished immune function, memory loss, fatigue, and a decreased sex drive. Some people pride themselves on how little sleep they need. Ask them how well that's working for them when they reach age sixty-five—if they reach it at all!

Without sleep we would die, and with less than optimal sleep we tend to die earlier. Neuroscientist and sleep expert Matthew Walker is direct: "Sleep is the single most effective thing we can do to reset our brain and body health each day—Mother Nature's best effort yet at contra-death."[23]

Recent research is moving away from fixed stages of sleep. With more sensitive measurements, scientists have found that different regions of the brain are in different states at the same time, and that brain activity can vary over milliseconds. But for our purposes it does help to understand sleep in these classic stages, so that we know which ones to target for lucid dreaming.

Sleep apnea is a serious sleep disorder in which breathing repeatedly stops and starts throughout the night. It's a silent killer, because it doesn't allow for deep restorative sleep. It's also underdiagnosed. An estimated twenty-two million Americans have sleep apnea, and about 80 percent of them don't know they have it. The missed diagnoses cost an estimated $150 billion annually in the United States alone for things like lost productivity, car accidents, and other mishaps. One in five adults has mild to moderate sleep apnea; one in fifteen has severe apnea. If left untreated, sleep apnea can contribute to heart disease, stroke, diabetes, dementia, weight gain, high blood pressure, obesity, and a host of other conditions. I treat sleep apnea in my clinical practice, and managing it can be a life changer, even lifesaver.

When it comes to sleep apnea, ignorance is not bliss. The sleep scientist William Dement says, "Sleep is one of the most important predictors for how long you will live—as important as whether you smoke, exercise, or have high blood pressure or cholesterol."[24] The next exercise will help you determine whether you should follow up with a doctor for diagnosis and treatment.

EXERCISE: Screening for Sleep Apnea

The following screening questions can help you assess the likelihood that you (or a loved one, if you are close enough to respond for them) are suffering from this potentially deadly condition. If you answer yes to a number of the following questions, make an appointment with a sleep doctor *immediately*.

- Have you ever been told you snore?   Yes _____ No _____

- Are you overweight?   Yes _____ No _____

- Do you wake up choking or gasping?   Yes _____ No _____

- Do you have diabetes or high blood pressure?   Yes _____ No _____

- Have you ever had an irregular heart rhythm?   Yes _____ No _____

- How likely are you to doze off while watching TV, sitting and reading, sitting inactive in a public place, while stopped for a few minutes in traffic, sitting and talking to someone, or sitting quietly after lunch (where you had no alcohol)?

_____

- If you're female, does your neck measure over 15 inches?   Yes _____ No _____

- If you're male, is your neck size over 16.5 inches?   Yes _____ No _____

REM Sleep

After time in stage three, we briefly come back up to stage two, then enter a new stage, REM sleep, or stage four. Again, this is when we dream the most. Our brain waves come back up from delta to alpha, which means the brain returns to daytime frequencies, and uses as much energy as when we're awake. After dreaming in REM sleep for some time, we have brief moments of awakening when we toss and turn. Then we go back down through the stages again, in four or five ninety-minute cycles each night (depending on how long we sleep).

Do you find yourself getting up a lot during the night? Tonight, take note of how many times you experience these micro-awakenings. In the morning, write down what you experienced.

_____

_____

_____

_____

_____

This exercise will help you develop a more refined understanding of your sleep patterns, which will be useful for lucid dreaming.

With each subsequent ninety-minute cycle, REM time roughly doubles. The end of a REM session, like the end of stage three non-REM, is often marked by a brief awakening. Some sleep scientists theorize that REM sleep is when we're the most insightful, intelligent, creative, and free. It's the playtime of the brain. Sleep researcher Michael Perlis writes, "REM sleep may be the one thing that makes us the most human, both for what it does for the brain and body, and for the sheer experience of it."[25]

The first REM period is only five to ten minutes, which is why we rarely remember dreams from early in the night (unless our sleep is interrupted). But as the night progresses, non-REM sleep is replaced with REM sleep, which means we spend more and more time dreaming as the night goes on.

The first half of the night is mostly non-REM sleep; the second half transitions into mostly REM. In the final sleep cycle of the night we can be in REM sleep for up to an hour, which is why we mostly remember dreams we had just before we wake up. This is prime dreamtime. It's the sweet spot where we will concentrate our efforts to have lucid dreams.

When do you tend to remember your dreams the most? _____

Does your experience resonate with these phases of sleep? _____

Once again, by understanding these stages and cycles we can see why lucid dreaming doesn't affect our rest. Since most restorative sleep occurs in stage three sleep (and we don't touch that), and dreams occur mostly in stage four (when the brain isn't resting anyway), this worry is largely unfounded.

QUESTIONS AND ANSWERS

Is sleep paralysis dangerous, or something to worry about?

Sleep paralysis is completely natural. It may feel threatening if you don't know what's happening, but it's totally harmless. Most lucid dreamers find the experience fascinating. But for those who don't know what is happening, it's a different story. In some extreme cases it can literally scare one to death. For a riveting account of these rare events, see the book *Sleep Paralysis: Night-Mares, Nocebos, and the Mind-Body Connection* by the medical anthropologist Shelley Adler.

What happens to sleep stages as we age?

As with many other aspects of life, changes to our sleep patterns are normal as we grow older. As people age, they tend to have a harder time falling asleep and more difficulty staying asleep. Total sleep time (TST) and the percentage of slow-wave sleep declines with age, while the percentages of stage one and stage two sleep increase. The need for sleep does not decline as we age, but the quality of sleep diminishes. But with good sleep hygiene (discussed in chapter 8), we still have a great deal of control over the quality of our sleep.

Does REM sleep also change as we age?

The relationship between age and the percentage of REM sleep is essentially linear in most adults, decreasing about 0.5 percent per decade up until the mid-seventies. After that time there is a small increase in the percentage of REM, due to REM time increasing while TST declines. However, as with much of science, there are other studies that report no age-related decline in REM sleep.

Does that mean that my chances of achieving lucidity decrease?

Not necessarily. These statistics apply to those who don't work on their dreams. Most people report an increase in lucid dreams if they continue to apply the methods and training for attaining lucidity.

Are the dreams we have in REM sleep different from those in non-REM?

Dreams reported during REM sleep tend to be more vivid and active, and more likely to be propelled by anxiety or fear. People report more nightmares during REM sleep. Non-REM dreams tend to be more pleasant and ordinary and less anxious. In REM dreams we also tend to play more active roles, while in non-REM dreams we tend to be passive observers of the dream.

Part II

How to Have
Lucid Dreams

CHAPTER 5

The Foundational Techniques

Lucid dreaming is similar to studying any other skill, be it playing the violin, learning tennis, or mastering a new language. You'll get out of it what you put into it. Can you expect to play golf like Tiger Woods in just a few weeks? Lucid dreaming is an art, and it helps if you treat it as such.

Think about other activities in which you are proficient, like sports, music, or crafts. How long did it take you to get good at that activity? Did you have to deal with discouragement, setbacks, and other challenges? Write about that here:

_____

_____

_____

_____

_____

Be reasonable in your expectations for lucid dreaming, as setting the bar too high may lead to disappointment. Humor also goes a long way, along with an attitude of curiosity and openness. In the meditative traditions there's a saying: "Not too tight, not too loose." If you are too ambitious, expect immediate results, and hope to master lucid dreaming in a few weeks, you're too tight. If your motivation is fuzzy, you don't really want to be bothered, and you apply the techniques flippantly, you'll get flippant results. You're too loose. You'll accomplish success in lucidity by tuning your mind and finding that sweet spot between tight and loose that makes for beautiful night music.

What are your expectations for lucid dreaming? Are you a bit tight, expecting instant results? Or are you somewhat loose, not really caring about results? Write your expectations here:

_____

_____

_____

Lucid dreaming can be tricky because it is a subtle practice. The dreaming mind is a quiet mind; in comparison, the daytime mind is loud. Learning how to silence ourselves is one secret to success in lucid dreaming. When darkness descends, and we don't drown it out with artificial light, the night invites a form of natural retreat. We retreat indoors and then further inside ourselves as we go to bed. We transition into being an introvert, which means "to turn to the inside." My task is to help you make that turn gracefully and lucidly.

Lucid dreaming is also a subtle practice because you have to become your own guide. I can hold your hand during the day, but no one can truly lead you into the dark. No one knows your sleep patterns, your mind, and your nighttime idiosyncrasies better than you. This is also what makes lucid dreaming so exhilarating. You're the one making the discoveries for yourself. You're the one blazing your own path to an entirely new way of sleeping and dreaming.

How do you feel about being your own guide? Does this intimidate you or excite you? Are you better off with guided meditations, or do you do well fending for yourself?

_____

_____

_____

In all the techniques in this book, trust your own experience and do what feels right for you.

Before we get into the specific induction methods, we need to understand a few basic approaches that underlie everything. These foundational techniques are often enough to spark lucidity. But even if they don't, they provide the foundation for every technique that follows. In the Buddhist tradition it is taught that the *preliminaries are more important than the main practice*. Set the proper stage, and the performance can begin.

I was teaching a meditation seminar a few years ago when I overheard a delightful lady, scurrying into the meditation room, say to herself, "C'mon, inner peace. I ain't got all day!" I often get the same vibe from my lucid dreaming participants: "C'mon, lucid dreaming. I ain't got all night!" But things of value sometimes do take all day or night. People these days are impatient. They rush to the goodies, and then wonder why things don't work. *Just give me the induction methods!* But if we skip over the foundational practices of this chapter, we lessen our chances of success. With these preliminary practices we're creating a field of dreams. "If you build it, they will come." When we plant seeds (the specific induction methods) in a field that has been weeded, tilled, watered, and fertilized, they will take root, grow, and flower. If we don't, it's like tossing seeds onto concrete.

THE POWER OF BELIEF

All the induction techniques are catalyzed by our *belief* in the technique and in lucid dreaming altogether. Our beliefs either hold us back or propel us forward. In the medical world, the power of belief is at the core of the placebo effect, which is really a belief effect. The medicinal effect can be delivered just by our believing in a medicine. The induction techniques in the following chapters are *not* sugar pills. They're real medicine, and they work. But belief turbocharges their effects.

In the world of lucid dreaming, we replace the popular saying "I'll believe it when I see it" with "I'll see it when I believe it." One reason we don't have lucid dreams is because we don't believe in the importance of dreaming. In Western societies, we're generally not trained to honor our dreams or to believe in them. This is why I spent so much time discussing the benefits of lucid dreaming—to make it more believable and important.

EXERCISE: Becoming a Believer

Take a few moments and reflect on where you stand with lucid dreaming.

How important are your dreams to you? _____

How important is it for you to start having lucid dreams? _____

What would it take for you to really believe in the power of lucid dreaming?

_____

_____

_____

_____

What kind of scientific and academic support might you need?

_____

_____

What kind of personal experience might you need?

_____

_____

_____

THE POWER OF INTENTION

The second foundational technique is *intention*. This is of such importance that in a recent dream yoga seminar I attended, given by a Tibetan master, intention was the *only* induction method he presented. He proclaimed that intention alone is enough to spark lucidity.

Intention is something you cultivate during the day but that reaches deep into the unconscious mind to pop up in your dreams. That ping of recognition is enough to flip a non-lucid dream into a lucid one, as easily as flipping on a light switch. The simplicity is part of the reason some people don't believe intention alone is enough. But it works exactly the same as setting the intention before you go to sleep that you absolutely must wake up at 3:00 a.m. to catch a flight. In the absence of an alarm clock, countless people have used the power of intention to wake themselves up in the dead of night. Setting a strong intention to become lucid in your dreams is almost as good as setting a literal alarm.

If you haven't had this "alarming" experience, try setting a fervent intention that you *must* get up at a 4:00 a.m. tonight (or whatever time you like). Really put your heart into it. As you go to sleep, reinstate this intention. Then the following morning, write down what you experienced.

_____

_____

_____

_____

EXERCISE: Setting Your Intention

To ramp things up, say to yourself throughout the day: *Tonight I'm going to have many dreams; I'm going to have good dreams; I'm going to remember my dreams; I'm going to wake up within my dreams!* The wording isn't that important; it's the *feeling* that counts. Or make up your own motivational mantra here:

_____

_____

_____

Whatever phrase you come up with, don't just think it. Say it out loud and really mean it. Then write it down. Get it into your system. When you go to sleep, reset this "alarm." Recite your mantra at least twenty-one times during the day, then seven times when lying down to sleep. The momentum of these recitations carries the intention deep into your unconscious mind and therefore deep into the night. If you wake up during the night, reset your intention to wake up in your dreams. Then the next morning, write down what you experienced. If you didn't experience anything, write that down.

_____

_____

_____

_____

_____

I've taught many lucid dreaming seminars where people finally have a lucid dream, and because they're so excited they immediately wake up. They come to me thrilled that they had a lucid dream, but disappointed that it was so short. I'll inquire about their intent, and a typical response is, "My intention was to have a lucid dream." Well, you got what you asked for. Now ask for more.

Add something like this: *I want to have a lucid dream so that I can plunge into the depths of the ocean and swim with the dolphins, or soar into outer space and dance in the clouds! I want to experience the thrill of flying, to feel the wind blowing through my hair, and the excitement of swooping down close to the earth!* As any fundraiser will tell you, it's amazing what you can get if you just ask for it.

In the space provided, write down your new level of intention, and be specific. Put your heart into it. Visualize it. Feel into it. What do *you* want to do in your lucid dreams?

_____

_____

_____

_____

We'll return to the power of intention when we discuss the Eastern induction methods, where we'll see that intention is the central player behind karma.

THE POWER OF MEDITATION

Our third foundational technique is meditation. One big reason we're not lucid to our dreams at night is that we're not lucid to the contents of our mind during the day. What is found now is found then. Or more precisely, what is *not* found now is *not* found then. We're unaware of—that is, we are non-lucid to—most of what occurs in our mind in our waking hours. It's no wonder we're non-lucid to our dreams.

For those who like logic: dreams are to dreaming consciousness as thoughts are to waking consciousness. If we become lucid to our thoughts during the day, we'll naturally become more lucid to our dreams at night. Stephen LaBerge says that waking consciousness is dreaming consciousness with sensory constraints; dreaming consciousness is waking consciousness without sensory constraints. The point being that it's the same consciousness at work, day or night, and therefore the same level of lucidity or non-lucidity.

EXERCISE: Lost in Thoughts

Pause and take an honest look at your mind. Is it jam-packed with endless thoughts? Are you aware of most of these thoughts, or do they race by undetected?

_____

_____

Most of what takes place in the average mind occurs without awareness. It's like watching CNN. There's the main story on the screen, but underneath it is the constant crawl of other news. We have a steady undercurrent of subconscious thought that streams by non-lucidly, and this is precisely why we have a constant current of non-lucid dreams. *We get lost in dreams the same way we get lost in thoughts.* We can see this when we drift away into a daydream, which is a beautifully descriptive term for this process of getting caught up and swept away. When a thought or an emotion pops up and we get sucked into it, that's non-lucidity.

Do you recognize this state of mind? If you've tried meditation or other awareness techniques before, describe your experience:

_____

_____

_____

_____

_____

The practice of meditation is therefore the practice of lucidity. This is why, as studies have shown, meditators have more lucid dreams. And for a meditation master, *all* their dreams are lucid. This is only natural, because meditation masters are lucidity masters, or masters of awareness.

We've defined lucid dreaming, but what exactly is lucid *thinking*? A lucid thought is one that you are aware of. In contrast, a non-lucid thought is one that arises without your awareness. With a lucid thought, you recognize that you're thinking, which instantly transforms a non-lucid thought into a lucid one. You're still thinking, but now you know it.

Meditation has a unique role in lucid dreaming because it's simultaneously diagnostic and prescriptive. It shows us why we have so many non-lucid dreams and what we can to do to start having lucid ones. I've been meditating for over forty years and can attest to the truth of these claims. When I go into retreat and meditate most of the day, my lucid dreams come to life at night. When my meditation practice tapers off, my lucid dreams do as well.

Recall that a non-lucid dream is a mindless dream, a distracted dream, a forgotten dream, and that a lucid dream is a mindful dream, a non-distracted dream, a remembered dream. With the following meditation we're going to exercise mindfulness, non-distraction, and memory. Lucidity is a natural consequence of this exercise.

MEDITATION INSTRUCTION

There are many forms of meditation, and many ways to present it. The best approach is to keep it simple. In over thirty years as a meditation instructor, I often teach the following mindfulness meditation in three phases: the body phase, the breath phase, and the mind phase. We start with the ground, with our physical posture, and work our way up. Most of the instruction deals with this first phase, which reinstates our theme that the preliminaries (body phase) are more important than the main practice (the mind phase). As one meditation master put it, "Simply by taking the proper posture in meditation, sooner or later you will find yourself meditating." It's also akin to our "field of dreams" narrative. If you build it (good posture), mindfulness (lucidity) will come.

EXERCISE: Instant Meditation

To give you a sense of the power of posture, close your eyes for a minute and simply notice the quality of your mind. Don't change a thing. By inviting the smallest shift in posture, you're going to change the quality of your mind. Smile. Simply raise the corners of your lips a few millimeters. Write down what you notice.

_____

_____

_____

Does your mind smile when your body smiles?

_____

Paul Ekman, a pioneer in the study of emotions and facial expressions, noticed that when he assumed a facial expression of depression, he found himself getting depressed. Your body is not the same as your mind, but it's also not different. We're going to employ this traditional claim and use good physical posture to invoke good mental posture. A lucid body invites a lucid mind.

The Body Phase

Before we take our seat in meditation, we start with the proper mental posture or attitude. Take your seat on a floor cushion with a sense of dignity and confidence (minor adjustments for sitting in a chair will be offered as well). Assume the attitude of *I can do this!* Adopt a feeling of nobility, even regalness, like you're about to take command of the world.

Cross your legs naturally and feel the quality of being grounded on this good earth. Rest your hands on your thighs, not too far forward (which will tip you forward) and not too close to your torso (which will tip you back). It's the "middle way" theme again, or "not too tight, not too loose." Feel your spine centering itself, upright, firm, but not stiff. A strong back represents the quality of fearlessness and strength. An attitude that nothing can move you.

This is balanced with an open front, or exposed heart, which represents the quality of gentleness and receptivity. These two qualities of fearlessness and gentleness are also the key qualities for the mind phase of instruction—which is about developing a gentle but fearless relationship with the contents of your mind. The instructions for each phase are mixed with the instructions for the other phases. This is another instance of our theme of bidirectionality, or in this case tridirectionality: body, breath, and mind all working to support each other.

Good posture usually means allowing your chest to be open and exposing your heart. In Sanskrit and Pali, "mind" and "heart" come from the same root, *citta*. So "mindfulness" also means "heartfulness." This is important, because people tend to think of mindfulness as a purely cognitive event. But it's just as much an embodied or a heartful event. In the spirit of stealth help, by working with your body in this way you are already working with your mind, whether you know it or not.

A core instruction for meditation is to open your heart and mind. Everything hinges on this instruction. This aligns with my favorite definition of meditation: "habituation to openness." Open heart means open mind, and a sturdy but open posture invites this.

As a further refinement for the body phase, part your lips as if you're whispering the word "Ah," and gently rest the tip of your tongue against the back of your upper teeth. This helps to prevent excess salivation. Finally, keep your eyes open, with your gaze down about six feet in front of you. It's a receptive, unfocused, and *open* visual field, which invites the mind's eye to assume a similar open gaze. If this doesn't feel right, you can close your eyes. See which works best for you.

We'll adapt these instructions for sleep when we learn how to meditate while lying down, which is when we will close our eyes. I invite you to keep your eyes open at this point because this echoes the spirit of openness. It's a bit more advanced than the closed-eye approach, but practicing with your eyes open helps you mix your meditation with post-meditation. Remember, lucid dreaming eventually leads to lucid living, and practicing with your eyes open facilitates that.

EXERCISE: Exploring the Body for Meditation

Let your chest be open with your shoulders gently back; allow your head to float easily above your spine, and open your heart. Now write what you feel.

_____

_____

_____

_____

Is this easy for you to do, or is there some hesitation? Do you feel too exposed, open, and vulnerable?

_____

Now totally collapse your posture. Slump your shoulders forward and let your head droop. Journal what you feel now.

_____

_____

_____

_____

Is this easier to do? Do you feel less exposed? For many people, it's easier to cave in and collapse into a more familiar "non-lucid" posture. Notice the resistance to any phase of these instructions, and journal it.

_____

_____

_____

_____

Then be kind to yourself. Smile at what you discover. Realize that even with your body it takes time to open up. Finally, sit in meditation with your eyes closed for a few minutes, then open your eyes. Which one feels better? And why does it feel better?

_____

_____

_____

_____

Meditation on a chair is an option; just make sure it isn't too hard or too soft. Plant your feet solidly on the ground and feel that connection to the earth. Rest your hands on your thighs, as directed for the cross-legged posture. Don't lean against the back of the chair. This symbolizes that you can do this on your own, without any additional support. Continue with the original instructions.

If you have physical discomfort, like an itch or some pain, relate to that discomfort for a few moments before doing what you need to do to get comfortable. Stretch your legs, bring your knees up, scratch, or whatever. When the discomfort subsides, resume the posture. The idea of "fresh start" is helpful in meditation. If things are feeling stale, or not quite right, let the whole thing crumble for a minute. Then start afresh.

The Breath Phase

After establishing a good posture, bring your awareness to the natural movement of your breathing. Don't imagine it, don't think about it, just feel it. Let your mind ride the natural movement of your breath, which is the movement of life itself.

With phase one, the body, and phase two, the breath, you're simply sitting and breathing. That's it. But you're doing so fully and completely. When people ask me what we do at my meditation center, I'll often reply, "We do nothing. But we do it really well." It's not so easy to do nothing, because we're human *doings* more than human beings. How often do we say to ourselves and others, "I've got so much to do!"

Every time a thought or an emotion pulls us into doing something, a tug we'll soon feel in meditation, we're feeling the tug of non-lucidity. In other words, to be fully present with our body and our breath—*with what's really happening*—is what it means to be lucid. It's like the stipulation for many raffles: "You must be present to win." To wake up in our dreams means to be fully present in our dreams, to what's happening. We must be present to be lucid.

EXERCISE: The Mind-Breath Connection

To explore the connection between mind and breath, take about twenty rapid, shallow breaths and notice how this affects your mind. Write down what you experience.

_____

_____

_____

Now take a few slow, deep breaths, then write down how this affects your mind.

_____

_____

Finally, hold your breath for as long as you comfortably can, and journal what that does.

_____

_____

Do you notice any relationship between the frequency of your breathing and the frequency of your thoughts?

_____

The Mind Phase

This third phase is all about relating to your mind. When a thought or any other mental content arises—an image, regret, fantasy, anticipation, and so on—you'll mentally say to yourself *wake up* as an act of recognition that your mind has strayed from your body and breath. This *wake up* is not a reprimand, but an act of recognition—an act of lucidity. The reminder is gentle but precise, like popping a bubble with a feather. You're not trying to get rid of your thoughts or somehow stop the natural play of your mind. The mind just thinks. That's not a problem. The problem is an inappropriate relationship to your thoughts. Grasping after thoughts or pushing them away is the problem. In our terms, non-lucidity is the problem.

When you first start to practice, it's common to tell yourself *wake up* all the time. It's almost like a mantra initially, because there's so much thinking going on. But eventually the mind settles down. Thoughts, images, and the like still arise, but they're no longer bumper-to-bumper. Instead of one thought tailgating the next, some space starts to appear between your thoughts. You notice the thoughts earlier, and you become lucid to them sooner.

EXERCISE: Noticing

Tomorrow morning, before your day gets going, sit in meditation for ten minutes. Then, like a good reporter writing a travelogue, journal what you notice.

What's the "traffic" like first thing in the morning? Is your mind fresher and more spacious, less speedy, earlier in the day?

Place your hand over your heart as a gentle way to check in with yourself. What's the "weather" like inside? Is it sunny, cloudy, or stormy?

Whatever the climate is inside, it's okay. You're okay. Holding your hand over your heart gives you permission to be yourself. Accept the weather of your mind just as it is.

At the end of your day, sit in meditation for ten minutes. How is your mind different now?

_____

_____

Are you speedier, more stressed? Do you feel how the momentum of your day affects the state of your mind in the evening?

_____

_____

This type of noticing will help you understand how your activities and states of mind naturally extend into your meditation and eventually into your dreams. It's important to understand that your morning session isn't any *better* than your evening session. At both times, you're "becoming familiar with" (the very definition of meditation) how your mind plays out and learning to stay open to that play. Acceptance is a core ingredient in meditation. Stormy, rainy, or sunny, it's all going to blow through. The yoga master Swami Kripalu said, "The highest form of spiritual practice is self-observation without judgment."

By this point you're probably catching on that "to become familiar with" translates in our terms as "to become lucid to." Again, the more familiar we become with our mind, the more lucid we are to its display—day or night.

Heightened Contrast

The body and breath phases of meditation act like a canvas, a background of stillness, that allows us to better observe—and therefore become lucid to—the movement of our mind. In the tantric tradition, thoughts are actually referred to as the "movement of mind." During the day, the incessant movement of our mind is camouflaged by the incessant movements of our body and speech (speech is an aspect of the breath phase). We're constantly moving or talking. By sitting down and shutting up, we remove the camouflage. Speech reduces into breath, bodily movement reduces into stillness, and the mind now stands out. It's similar to what happens when we lie down to go to sleep. But in the case of sitting meditation, we're allowing the mind to stand out so we can better see it and become lucid to it.

This is why many beginning meditators complain that meditation is making things worse. "I never had so many thoughts before!" Yes you did. You just never saw them before. You were never lucid to them before.

I recommend that you start with ten minutes a day. The more the better, but the "middle way" approach is sound. Don't set your bar too high, but also remember that a little stretching is good for growth. Mornings are always good, but you can practice at any time. Because I'm fanatical about lucidity, I start and finish every day with meditation. It's the most important thing I do.

Sitting meditation is disarmingly simple. Surrender to that simplicity. Don't try to outsmart it. The profundity of this practice comes from its simplicity.

QUESTIONS AND ANSWERS

You say that with lucid dreaming you become your own guide. But what about those who talk about "dream guides" or other forms of assistance in the dream world?

As a general rule, our journey during the night is a solitary one. Once we learn the techniques, we can surely do it by ourselves. But for those who believe in guides or supernatural help, these can help. The great Swiss psychologist Carl Jung first met his spirit guide Philemon, the archetype of a wise old man, in his dreams. But even Jung intimated that this seemingly outer guru was but a representation of inner wisdom. "[Philemon] was simply a superior knowledge, and he taught me psychological objectivity and the actuality of the soul. He formulated and expressed everything which I had never thought." While I don't have such a specific guide, I do recite a short prayer every night that opens me up to "outside" assistance. Once again, if this sort of thing works for you, use it. If it doesn't, you don't really need it.

I have a hard time believing that intention and belief alone can spark lucidity. Is it really that simple?

This is where you have to trust me, and countless other teachers, when we confidently proclaim that these simple approaches alone can lead to lucid dreams. But simple doesn't always mean easy. We live in a culture that doesn't honor dreams, and that dismissive attitude has infected us. It's a form of poverty mentality, a subconscious attitude of *You can't do it!* It's sad that studies continue to show that the negative outplays the positive. Neuropsychologist Rick Hanson writes, "It's easy to acquire feelings of learned helplessness from a few failures, but hard to undo those feelings, even with many successes."[26] In relationships, it generally takes five positive interactions to overcome the effects of one negative act. In life overall, people do more to avoid a loss than to acquire a comparable gain.

Isn't meditation a Buddhist thing? I'm not interested in practicing Buddhism or any other religion.

While meditation is part of the Buddhist tradition (and many others), it is not essentially religious, or even spiritual. People often conflate meditation with spirituality and religion, but upon examination anyone can see that meditation is neither. Was there anything religious or spiritual in the instructions I've provided? Meditation is about working with the human mind. It is about becoming familiar with it, relating to it, opening to it, empowering it, and becoming increasingly lucid to its contents. Meditation is an inner technology. It is fundamentally neutral. But like any technology, meditation can be used in many different ways, some of which are spiritual or religious. We're using it to cultivate lucidity. There are over six thousand scientific studies showing the benefits of meditation for your body and your mind, none of which address spiritual or religious concerns.

There are times in meditation when I just can't stay awake. What should I do?

This is a common issue, and easily handled. When the mind starts to slow down in meditation, we tend to associate that quiescence with sleep, so we start to doze off. This is often a result of being "too loose." To counteract this droopiness, open your eyes (if they've been closed) and raise your gaze. Keep your vision unfocused, but open yourself up to more sensory stimulation. Tighten your posture, which means straightening your back. You will often notice that you're starting to slump as your mind slumps. If that doesn't do it, then take a few extra deep breaths, infusing your body with fresh oxygen. If *that* doesn't do it, then give yourself a break and take a nap.

Sometimes my mind just feels crazy. I can't seem to control it, and I tie myself into knots!

Meditation isn't about "mind control" in the traditional sense. You're not trying to muscle your mind into place; that would be way too tight. You're trying to establish or control a more sane and lucid relationship to it. If your mind is racing, just take a walk on the wild side, as Lou Reed sang. Sit back and watch the display—but without allowing yourself to get sucked into it. Appreciate and even celebrate what your mind can do. *Wow, look at all these thoughts! Amazing!* This shift in relationship can have a dramatic effect and help you relate to your "insanity" in a very sane way. So what if your mind is wild? Don't be afraid of the wilderness inside. Be an intrepid explorer and delight in that. So what if it's a bit "windy" inside today? Go fly a kite. This approach can also be used to relate to insomnia in a new way. With insomnia, the mind is in a similarly uncaged state, free from the constraints of physical distraction. If your mind is racing in your meditation, try closing your eyes (if they were open), lowering your gaze, and relaxing your posture. See what that does. A key to success is being kind to yourself. We do need to try—otherwise we're not meditating, we're just vegetating. But don't try too hard. Find that middle ground between too tight and too loose.

I just can't seem to stop my thoughts. Does this mean meditation just isn't for me?

Meditation is not about stopping your thoughts. This cannot be overstated. The only thing it stops is an inappropriate relationship to your thoughts. In decades as a meditation instructor, the most common problem I see is not with meditation; rather, it's with our definitions of meditation. People bring a host of preconceptions of what meditation is, and they impose those complex ideas onto an extremely simple practice. That's where the problems begin. So refine your understanding of meditation, which is largely accomplished by just doing it.

Can you really learn how to meditate from a book?

Can you learn to play golf, or the violin, by reading a book? Yes and no. The foundations can be presented, the view and philosophy articulated, but it obviously helps to have live instruction. With the mindfulness revolution in full swing, there are many self-proclaimed meditation instructors. Take your time in finding one; ask the tough questions, ask to talk to some of their other students (references), ask for credentials and any level of certification. There are great instructors out there, but just as many dilettantes.

CHAPTER 6

Western Daytime Induction Techniques

With these preliminaries behind us, we have prepared our field of dreams. Now it's time to plant the seeds. In the following chapters, I will give you the best daytime and nighttime techniques from the East and the West. The point is not to master them all or even to try them all. The point is lucidity, not the technique that gets you there. These different methods are presented because we're all different. Lucid dreaming is not a "one size fits all" practice. One technique may work well for you but not for your friend. Some people will connect with the Western techniques, others with the Eastern methods. You might also find that different techniques work at different times. I offer the variety of induction methods for you to tailor fit the practice for yourself.

Are you the kind of person that wants to be closely guided in a new venture? Or do you thrive when you can blaze your own way?

Either approach works with lucid dreaming. If you want to be told what to do, concentrate on the first techniques presented here. If you want to forge your own path, see which of the following methods speaks to you, and experiment with a variety of techniques. These alternative approaches will help you relax when you see how many techniques are available.

Once you find a method that works, stick with it. That's your ticket in. There's no need to do any of the others, unless you want to become a teacher or a well-rounded expert. I recommend that you stick with one method for at least several weeks to give it a chance. If you hop around from one technique to another too quickly, it's possible nothing will work. However, even if you spread your effort across a number of techniques, all the attempts you make to become lucid add up. Sooner or later, buoyed by your strong intent, the accrued efforts will push open the door to lucidity.

Just by trying to have lucid dreams, you're starting to change your relationship to the dream world and therefore to your unconscious mind. You're opening that two-way street between your conscious and unconscious mind, and beneficial information can now begin to flow. So while it may not seem like anything is happening at first, something *is* happening. It's simply occurring below the surface, beneath your conscious mind.

Is this already happening for you? Are you starting to notice your dream world shifting? What changes have you noticed since you started reading this book?

_____

_____

_____

_____

Attaining lucidity is like heating up a big pot of cold water. The cold water represents a lifetime of non-lucid dreams, and the heat represents the amount of energy you put into your practice. At first nothing seems to be happening. You're doing the practices but nothing seems to be working. Then one day bubbles start rising in the water, and you have your first lucid dream. All that effort was heating up the pot. So by merely trying, you're getting warm.

This is important to understand because it's easy to get discouraged. The secret to success is determination and perseverance. As the Dalai Lama says of anything worthwhile: "Never give up!"

Do you feel like you're getting warm? Or is your experience still pretty cold? If it is cold, what do you think you need to do to heat things up?

_____

_____

INCREASING DREAM RECALL

We have four or five dream sessions (REM periods) every night. This means there are at least four chances to become lucid every night. Some people say they don't dream, which really means they don't remember their dreams. So the first thing we need to do is increase our dream recall. As one teacher told me, "No dreams, no lucid dreams." If you already remember several dreams each night, you can skip this section.

How many dreams do you remember each night? Have you noticed any changes in dream recall since you started reading this book?

_____

_____

Have you noticed any increase in recall since you started meditating?

_____

_____

Good dream recall begins with a good attitude and your *belief* in the importance of dreams. If you don't value your dreams, you will dismiss them. So enhance your relationship to dreams altogether by reading more about the topic, listening to podcasts and TED talks, and attending seminars. If you make your dreams important, they will come to you more frequently. Dream researcher Patricia Garfield writes, "Those who do not 'believe in' dreams or who believe them to be nonsense do not remember their dreams or have only nonsensical ones. Dreams are what you make of them...dream states respond to waking attitudes."[27]

Next, harness the power of intention by resolutely telling yourself that you *will* remember your dreams. Put your heart into it. Get plenty of sleep, and allow yourself to sleep in. Part of the fun of lucid dreaming is giving yourself permission to languish in bed and take full advantage of prime time dreamtime.

EXERCISE: Building Your Dream Recall

If you're having a hard time remembering your dreams, write down any snippet of any dream you can remember. When you wake up, either during the night or at the end of your sleep in the morning, ask yourself, *Was I just dreaming?* Close your eyes and try to recapture any part of the dream. Pick up the scent and follow it. And if you can remember (this comes with practice), *don't move.* Moving engages waking consciousness and pulls you out of the dream world. If you've already moved, and you sense that you did have a dream, return to the position you were in when you first woke up. Memories are lodged in our bodies, and by returning to that position you may find yourself returning to a dream. Try flopping slowly from side to side, and see if that jogs loose the memory of a dream.

Write down your experience with this exercise. Does staying still and looking within help you recapture your dreams? Does moving mindfully from side to side in the morning help?

_____

_____

_____

Here's a daytime practice to support dream recall. Set a timer or some other trigger to go off at random times throughout the day. When it goes off, pause and try to recall the thoughts you were thinking from the past minute. If you catch yourself in moments of reverie or daydreaming, mentally backtrack and try to recapture the images. This is another bidirectional, or reciprocating, practice. What you do during the day will help what you do at night, and vice versa.

Try this practice for the next week, and write down what you experience. Are you able to recall the thoughts you were thinking prior to the timer going off? Or is it difficult to pick up the scent?

_____

_____

_____

This practice is simultaneously preparatory and revelatory. It will prepare you for better dream recall and reveal how much or little you remember now. As you progress through the book, use the space here to log how this exercise changes for you. Is your memory improving as you exercise it?

_____

_____

_____

_____

STATE CHECKS

One of the main reasons we don't recognize that we're dreaming while we're dreaming is because we don't question the status of our dream experience. We blindly accept whatever happens, no mater how weird it is. A fire-spitting dragon walks in front of you, and you just go along with it. You're flying with the eagles and heedlessly accept that as your reality. Your deceased father appears at the front door, and you take that as normal. This naïve acquiescence, or going along with things as they appear, is the essence of non-lucidity. By accepting things at face value, you remain stuck in a non-lucid dream.

Does this describe your dreams? Do you just go with the flow of what's happening, no matter how bizarre it is? Have you ever questioned the status of your dreams?

_____

_____

Conducting a state check, or reality check, is about developing a more critical attitude toward your experience. We start the practice during the day, then extend it into our dreams. In the world of lucid dreaming, you want to Question Authority, just like the bumper sticker says. You want to challenge the normally uncontested authority of whatever appears. By doing state checks, you're checking to see what state of consciousness you are in. Are you awake or dreaming?

EXERCISE: The Art of the State Check

The practice is simple. Whenever anything strange, out of the ordinary, or dreamlike happens during the day, perform a state check. There are many ways to do this. Look at the palm of your hand. Now move your hand out of your line of vision, then place it in front of you again. Do it right now.

Does your hand appear the same the second time you look at it, or is it different?

_____

If your palm appears the same way, that suggests that you're awake. But if you bring your hand back into sight and you now have six fingers, or your thumb is green, or a finger has fallen off, or the size has changed, you're dreaming (or on drugs). Do this, or any of the other state checks that follow, at least five times a day. Get into the habit of conducting state checks now, and that habit will naturally extend into your dreams.

Here are a few more. If you have a digital watch, look at it. Now move it out of sight, then move it back into view. If things look the same, you're awake. But if something overtly changes with the watch, you're dreaming. Even though it feels contrived, bring your watch into sight, pull it away, and move it back in. Is the watch the same or different the second time you look at it?

_____

My favorite state check is also the easiest. Just stand and jump up, feet leaving the ground. If you come back down, you're awake. But if you keep going up, or drop down and fall through the earth, you're dreaming. So even if you're sitting down, jump up right now. As you go about your day, jump up at least five times every day and see what happens. The more you do it, the stronger the habit becomes.

Come up with your own state checks—ways to test whether you're awake or dreaming—and write them down here. Even thinking about new state checks will help you relate to waking and dreaming states in a more sensitive way.

_____

_____

The idea is to sensitize yourself to the odd things that happen throughout the day, and to then carry out a reality check. For example, the next time a book falls off the shelf, jump up and see if you come back down. The next time a bird thumps into your window, a neighbor's pet strays into your garage, a light bulb pops, conduct a state check. The next time the president dogs bird into yesterday's garbage can—or any other nonsensical event occurs—do your check.

For the next few days (or, if you're serious about lucid dreaming, for the rest of your life), write down all the dreamlike events that happen to you. Journal these bizarre or incongruous events here:

_____

_____

_____

_____

_____

By conducting state checks during the day, you will begin to check the status of your reality when you dream. *Hey, wait a minute—my father is not alive,* or *I can't fly in real life. I must be dreaming!* And you're instantly lucid. It's a way to use the power of habit in your favor. Instead of the bad habit of constantly going along with the (non-lucid) flow, you're instilling the good habit of checking your state of consciousness.

Once you get the hang of this practice, your increased sensitivity will detect more and more oddities and dreamlike events in your daily life. You're installing a new set of antennae that will pick up strange events during your day and send you the signal to test the status of your reality. This heightened awareness *is* a form of lucidity, and it will naturally extend into your dreams. In other words, the very practice of sensitizing yourself to be aware of oddities is itself the practice of lucidity, whether or not you conduct the state check. So it's another "twofer" practice. You're getting two benefits for the price of one.

You want to get to the point where conducting a state check becomes automatic every time you experience something strange. It's like conditioning yourself to say "Gesundheit!" when someone sneezes. I frequently jump up and down with my state checks throughout the day (my lucidity "gesundheit"), skipping my way into lucidity.

DREAMSIGNS

Working with dreamsigns, like conducting state checks, is all about installing those lucidity pop-ups that eventually ping into your dreams, clueing you in to the fact that you're dreaming. A dreamsign is any strange, disjointed, fluid, or otherwise dreamlike event that occurs during the day, like that book that suddenly falls, that bird hitting the window, and that strange cat walking into your garage. We've been talking about the daytime version of dreamsigns already, so this section shows you how to work with nighttime signs.

Start by writing down any recurrent dreams in the space provided at the end of this book. This is a long-term project that begins now. Then sensitize yourself to their common features. You can use a colored marker to highlight recurrent features. Note the recurring people, places, or images that arise in these repetitive dreams. Then study or even memorize them with the intent that the next time you encounter these recurring people, places, feeling tones, or images you will use them as signs that you're dreaming. Within a few weeks you'll have a list of dreamsigns that you can use to gain lucid awareness in your next dream. For example, you'll be able to tell yourself something like, *The next time my dead uncle (or other dead person) appears in my dream, I'll use that as a sign that I must be dreaming.* You can do the same with recurring themes in your dreams, like running through an airport to catch a flight, or skiing, or not being ready for that exam.

A lucid dreaming friend shared with me that she's had a recurring dream for decades about the home she grew up in along the shores of Lake Erie. Every time she dreams of that home, or of Lake Erie, she's conditioned herself to use those appearances as clues that she's dreaming. Sometimes she'll conduct a state check to confirm that she is dreaming, but it happens so often that she usually doesn't have to do that. The images of the house or the lake are enough to clue her in to the fact that she must be dreaming.

PROSPECTIVE MEMORY

Memory plays a big role in the world of lucid dreaming. A lucid dream is a dream in which you remember that you're dreaming. Non-lucidity is therefore a product of forgetfulness. You forget that you're dreaming when you're dreaming.

Most of our memory is retrospective, a recollection of the past. Prospective memory, however, is remembering to do something in the future. When you're trying to remember to wake up in a dream, which is a future event, you're working with prospective memory, which can be strengthened with some exercises. We've been covertly working with this form of memory in our discussion of dream-signs and state checks; now it's time to make it more overt.

The practice here is to remember to do a state check whenever a specified event occurs. In this case, it can be anything, not just a dreamsign.

EXERCISE: Putting State Checks into Practice

Take your pick from these options, using state checks that will come up often for you in your daily life. I recommend setting a new trigger event each day, to keep the exercise fresh.

For the rest of today, sensitize yourself that the next time you get a text message, you'll do a state check.

At night, write down how many times you remembered to do that today.   _____

Every time you look in a mirror, do a check. At night, write down how many times you remembered to do this.   _____

Use the trigger of hearing a siren; at the end of the day, write down how many times you were able to remember to conduct a state check.   _____

Conduct a state check every time you hear a dog bark.   _____
How did that go?

_____

Do a state check every time you walk through a door.   _____

Do a state check every time you open the fridge.   _____

Do a state check every time you hear a jet.   _____

You get the idea. If these triggers don't work for you, come up with your own and jot them down here:

_____

_____

_____

_____

We started strengthening our memory muscle with the practice of meditation. Every time we come back to our body and our breath in meditation and mentally say, *wake up*, that's a moment of recollection. This is such an important point that the word for mindfulness in Tibetan is *drenpa*, which means "to recollect." The word "memory" itself comes from the Latin *memor*, which means "mindful." If forgetfulness is the problem, then remembrance is the solution. Both the practice of meditation and the exercise of prospective memory help us to remember.

Strengthening our memory is just like any other form of exercise: it takes effort and patience. We don't go to the gym one time and lift a thousand pounds all at once. To build our muscles properly, we lift ten pounds a hundred times, or one pound a thousand times. Repetition and persistence are the keys to success.

Just as the resistance of going to the gym reveals how important physical fitness is to you, these practices will reveal how important lucidity is to you. Are you willing to "go to the gym" with these exercises? If not, why not?

_____

_____

VIDEO GAMING AND VIRTUAL REALITY

The psychologist Jayne Gackenbach has shown that playing video games before bedtime may give gamers an increased level of awareness and control in their dreams. It makes sense: video games and dreams both represent alternate realities, and plugging into the former can help you plug into the latter with greater lucidity. Spending time in an imaginary but controllable world prepares gamers to perceive their dream world through a similar lens. Gamers practice controlling their game environments, and that can translate into controlling their dreams.

If you're a gamer, have you noticed an improvement in your dream experience?

Gackenbach extended her research into virtual reality (VR) and came to similar conclusions. "All this points to one thing," Gackenbach says. "When you alter people's waking realities, their memory changes. The more you think you're in one reality, it alters your memory of other realities."[28] Virtual-reality devices can train those who use them to relate to any unreal situation with greater awareness. Martin Dresler, a professor of cognitive neuroscience in the Netherlands, says, "One of the strategies to increase lucid dreaming frequency is to engage more in dream-related thinking. So it's indeed plausible that engagement in dreamlike environments—like many virtual-reality programs are—increases lucid dreaming frequency."[29]

In preparation for a scientific study I coauthored with a cognitive neuroscientist, I had the chance to experience VR extensively. It is the closest daytime experience to lucid dreaming I've ever had. The first night after trying VR I had a lucid dream, and virtual reality continues to grease the skids into nighttime lucidity. Patrick McNamara, a neuroscientist and professor at Boston University, says, "By using a virtual-reality device, you are putting yourself into a brain state that is remarkably like the REM brain state: a simulation without correction by external input. So it's easy to recall similar brain states or simulations under those conditions."[30]

If you have the opportunity to try VR, I recommend it. When you try it, write down your experience, and notice any impact it has on your dream world.

QUESTIONS AND ANSWERS

Have modern sleep patterns affected how we dream, or remember our dreams?

It seems so. According to history professor Roger Ekirch, sleeping in one consolidated eight-hour block is a relatively recent phenomenon. Ekirch's research revealed that humans used to sleep over a period of around twelve hours, during which time people would sleep in the "first sleep of the night" for three or four hours, then wake up for two or three hours, then return for the "second sleep of the night" for another three or four hours. (See his masterful book, *At Day's Close: Night in Times Past*.) The work of psychiatrist Thomas Wehr at the National Institute of Mental Health supports this claim. (See *Waking Up to the Dark: Ancient Wisdom for a Sleepless Age*, by Clark Strand.) Modern consolidated sleep patterns may therefore interfere with our awareness of dreams, and hence dream recall.

Are memories literally stored in the body?

Yes. One remarkable confirmation is that people who have had organ transplants often report dreams that provide information about the donor's behaviors, appearance, habits, and other data the recipient could not have possibly known. Heart transplant recipients often demonstrate a "change of heart," and take on characteristics of the donor. Memories may be stored in neurons, but neurons are not only stored in the brain. When you have a "gut feeling" about something, it could be because your gut, sometimes called "the second brain," contains some 100 million neurons, more than either the peripheral nervous system or the spinal cord. This enteric nervous system engages more than thirty neurotransmitters, just like the brain, and 95 percent of the body's serotonin is actually found in the bowels. (Irritable bowel syndrome is sometimes called a "mental illness" of the second brain.[31]) The psychoneuroimmunologist Candace Pert went so far as to assert that your body *is* your unconscious mind.[32] So yes, memories are stored in the body.

I heard that it's hard to read when you're in a dream. If that's true, could you use that as a dreamsign?

Absolutely. It is hard to read in dreams, even when they are lucid. This is one reason I included the garbled sentence in the section on dreamsigns—so you can use your difficulty in reading as a dreamsign. This phenomenon may be due to the activation of the brain's right hemisphere when you're dreaming, and the deactivation of the normally dominant left hemisphere, which is involved in the processing of information in a sequential order. (The left hemisphere dominates during waking consciousness, and the right hemisphere takes over during dreaming.) This fact can also help you distinguish lucid dreams from out-of-body experiences (OBEs). Most OBEs are actually lucid or hyperlucid dreams. If you can read while in a seemingly disembodied and altered state, it could be a genuine OBE. But if you struggle when trying to read, it's probably a lucid dream.

What about using mind-altering drugs, like marijuana?

With recreational (and medicinal) marijuana now legal in many states, this is a common question. Marijuana, like alcohol, tends to suppress REM sleep and therefore our dreams. It also increases the time we spend in non-REM sleep, which means more time in this restorative state. However, cannabis increases right-hemispheric brain activity, which is generally more active in the dream state. Cannabis acts like a mild psychedelic and, like other similar agents, it shifts daytime reality into a more dreamlike state. In this regard, as we'll explore in more detail when we talk about the daily Eastern practice of *illusory form*, it could act to facilitate lucid dreams. This is one area where the jury is still out, and the verdict is different from person to person.

How about stronger psychotropic agents like psilocybin, DMT, or LSD?

Psychedelics are now making a legitimate comeback and may return to Schedule II status, which means doctors can begin prescribing them. (See *How to Change Your Mind: What the New Science of Psychedelics Teaches Us About Consciousness, Dying, Addiction, Depression, and Transcendence*, by Michael Pollan; and *Am I Dreaming? The New Science of Consciousness and How Altered States Reboot the Brain*, by James Kingsland.) Until psychedelics become legal again (and therefore regulated, which is a good thing—one never knows what one gets with unregulated drugs), these mind-altering substances remain in the shadows of Western culture. Drugs in the LSD family, which includes psilocybin and tryptamine, stimulate REM sleep. Anecdotal reports suggest that microdoses of these agents do seem to facilitate lucid dreams. Psilocybin and ayahuasca (the most commonly used form to deliver DMT—the "spirit molecule" dimethyltryptamine) are legal in a number of countries, where they are used in sacred rituals. These substances also seem to help trigger lucidity. Many people report that these agents increase the frequency and clarity of dreams. (See *Dreaming Wide Awake: Lucid Dreaming, Shamanic Healing, and Psychedelics*, by David Jay Brown for more.) Despite my conservative nature, I am increasingly convinced that there is a place for these substances—if used properly, under expert supervision, delivered by a regulated industry, and in the right setting. But that said, there is clearly the potential for abuse, which is why they remain illegal.

CHAPTER 7

Eastern Daytime Induction Techniques

The following techniques are more specifically Eastern and may not speak to everyone. Be your own guide and trust your experience. I've been a student of Eastern philosophy for over forty years, so the following techniques work for me. But I appreciate what the Dalai Lama often says when he teaches: "If you find what I have to say helpful, take it to heart. If you don't, throw it out the window."

Our first Eastern daytime induction method belongs to the collection of foundational practices, the methods that come together to create our field of dreams. These fundamental practices lay the foundation for the more specific induction methods to follow.

ENHANCE YOUR RELATIONSHIP TO DREAMS

The first daytime induction method is to elevate and enhance your relationship to your dreams. The induction method could be either Eastern or Western, but the East generally honors dreams more than the West. You can improve your relationship to dreams in many ways.

- First, read and study the vast literature that explores the dream world. Write down here the books that you'd like to read (see Suggested Reading for tips).

  _____

  _____

- Augment that study with the burgeoning literature on lucid dreaming and dream yoga. Make a list here of the lucid dreaming and dream yoga books that interest you.

  _____

  _____

- Listen to podcasts or take online courses.

- Hang out with like-minded people, either in person or via forums offered by websites like Night Club or Reddit.

- Pay more attention to the dreams you're already having.

- Engage in all the exercises in this workbook.

- Keep a dream journal.

Do all this and you'll be on your way to establishing your own dream culture. Remember, in the world of lucid dreaming, the old maxim "I'll believe it when I see it" is reversed; here, "I'll see it when I believe it" reigns supreme. So do what it takes to believe it.

Our second Eastern daytime induction method, which is slowly being adopted by the West, is meditation. With the help of the mindfulness revolution, meditation has found a home in the West. It also now belongs to both Eastern and Western methods for cultivating lucidity, and its importance cannot be overstated. The meditations in this book are subtle practices designed to match the subtlety of the dreaming mind. In the darkness of the night, it's hard to meet or recognize something you haven't met in the light of day. By "meeting" and becoming familiar with these subtle dimensions of mind during the day, you will start to recognize these subtle states in the form of lucid dreams.

Close your eyes and observe your mind for a moment. Some meditation masters recommend a one-breath meditation session. Pay attention to one inhalation and exhalation. That's it! And since that one went so well, try another. Then write down the effects of meditating for just two breaths.

_____

_____

_____

_____

KARMA

"Karma" is one of the most frequently used terms in the spiritual business, and it is commonly misunderstood. Though Westerners often use it flippantly, as a way to say "what goes around comes around," karma actually operates at the level of a physical law, like gravity. Karma literally means "action" and is the Eastern way of talking about the principle of cause and effect, or habit. Our habits are the effects of previous patterns of behavior, which in turn cause or condition future behavior.

Over the course of this workbook, we're replacing unconscious bad habits that bring about non-lucidity with conscious good habits that bring about lucidity. Whether we know it or not, all our daily lucidity practices work with the laws of karma. It's just an Eastern way of saying, "You will get out of it what you put into it."

Proximate karma is a karmic law based on the fact that a succeeding state of consciousness is conditioned by the immediately preceding state. It's fairly obvious. For example, if you go to sleep all stressed out, you're setting yourself up for stressed-out dreams. Whereas if you go to sleep in a more meditative state, you're setting yourself up for more peaceful and lucid sleep. What we do just before sleep perfumes our dreams.

If you look closely at your world, you will see how the laws of karma or habit play out in it. Then you'll appreciate how you can harness these natural forces to work for your benefit. In Buddhism, sleep (which includes dreams) is called a "variable mental factor," which means it's either positive, negative, or neutral depending on how it is conditioned. And this conditioning largely depends on the immediately preceding state of mind. Sleep is like tofu in that it is fundamentally tasteless, a blank slate. The flavor comes from what you soak it in. With the following techniques we're going to marinate our mind in the secret sauces of lucidity.

ILLUSORY FORM

The daily practice of *illusory form* is one of the greatest contributions from the world of dream yoga. Illusory form is such a central practice that, in many classic texts, dream yoga (and therefore lucid dreaming) is considered a subset of illusory form. The practice is simple, but don't let the simplicity fool you.

Throughout the day, as often as you can, say to yourself, "This is a dream," or "I'm dreaming." By repeating this "mantra" throughout the day, and by examining the illusory nature of your waking life, you'll be more likely to notice the illusory nature of dreams while sleeping, and thereby spark a lucid dream.

Lucid dreaming and the practice of illusory form are reciprocating practices. The more you practice illusory form, the more lucid dreams you will have; and the more lucid dreams you have, the more you strengthen your practice of illusory form. In the spirit of bidirectionality, they "bootstrap" each other, or lift each other up. Because the practice is so simple, you can supplement it with the following exercises.

EXERCISE: **Persistent Reminders**

Put sticky notes around your house—in drawers, cabinets, or other places you visit often—to help you remember to do this practice throughout the day. You'll open your cereal cabinet and be greeted by the reminder, "This is a dream." Reach into the glove compartment, and "I'm dreaming" will be waiting for you. Illusory form is actually a spiritual practice, and the essence of spiritual practice is remembrance. Can you think of creative places to post these notes? Write those places down here, and post your notes in those locations today.

_____

_____

_____

_____

EXERCISE: **Only a Dream**

Say "This is a dream" aloud, not just mentally. The verbal recitation strengthens the karmic force. In Eastern thought, karma gets heavier when it goes from mental to verbal to physical. So put your heart into it. Try to *feel* into the notion that what you're perceiving is a dream. Now pause for a moment, look around, and repeat the mantra "This is a dream" for a few minutes. Really mean it. Then journal what you notice. Does your world get a little less solid? Does it actually start to feel more like a dream?

_____

_____

_____

_____

EXERCISE: Today Is Yesterday

Look at today from the perspective of tomorrow. Yesterday seemed so solid when you lived it, but from the perspective of today it's only as solid as a memory—or a dream. When you reflect back on today's events from tomorrow's perspective, today will appear more illusory. What does that feel like? Journal what you experience.

_____

_____

_____

_____

_____

EXERCISE: A Waking Dream

Transpose the characteristics of your dreams into your waking life. For example, most dreams are highly visual and disjointed. So do things like wear earplugs during the day, which invokes dreamlike states of mind. Or, when you blink, close your eyes a bit longer than usual, which will make your world disjointed. Write down what you experience.

_____

_____

_____

_____

_____

EXERCISE: Mirror Image

Look at things as they are reflected in a mirror, then look directly at the things being reflected. The mirror-like nature of things is a common teaching in illusory form texts. Do this for a few minutes and see if it shifts the way you perceive things. Write about this below.

_____

_____

_____

_____

_____

Do you feel any resistance to these practices? Do you find them patronizing, even silly? Is there part of you that doesn't want to see things as illusory? Write down what you notice.

_____

_____

EXERCISE: My Own Induction Methods

Once you get the hang of these illusory form practices, you can invent your own. Write down some of your own ways of seeing the illusory nature of things:

_____

_____

_____

SIMHA POSE

The *simha* pose, or sitting lion posture, comes from the Hindu Kriya Yoga tradition and works with the subtle body, a topic we will explore in chapter 9. It's a simple technique that works for many yoga practitioners. The first time I tried it I had a lucid dream that night. (Admittedly, this is anecdotal evidence, but I was impressed.)

EXERCISE: The Lion's Roar

Sit on your haunches like a lion: kneel down and rest your buttocks on your heels, either with the tops of your feet against the floor or, if that's uncomfortable, propped up on your flexed toes. Keep your back straight. With your hands, form the "fist of nonaggression," with your thumbs tucked inside your curled-up fingers (if you were to punch someone with this fist, you could break your thumb—hence the nonaggression name). Rest the heels of your palms on your thighs. You're like a proud and fearless lion surveying the savannah.

In this posture, you're going to take a deep breath, tip your head back, and roar like a lion, opening your fists and splaying out your fingers as you do so. Take this posture now, and roar at least three times. As you inhale between these three breaths, close your fists again; as you exhale, splay your fingers out again. Write down what you experience.

_____

_____

_____

_____

_____

Did you notice how your throat is stimulated by this exercise? We'll soon see that the throat chakra is integral to dream yoga and is used in a number of ways to induce lucid dreams. Give your lion another roar—and see what happens tonight. You may want to tell your family in advance that you're going to be doing this one!

MEDITATION AND MORAL CONDUCT

In Eastern traditions, meditation is always held in a larger social and cultural context of ethics and morality. In the West, meditation is often separated from this background and used as a stand-alone technique for everything from improving athletic performance to reducing stress. The fact that meditation has so many beneficial side effects attests to its power. But the ancient traditions that gave birth to meditation didn't design it to relieve stress or improve athletic performance.

If meditation is a foundational technique for lucidity—and you are starting to *believe* that—you will practice meditation better if you understand it better. Meditation itself abides by the *Field of Dreams* narrative: if you create the proper field for meditation, it will take root. So this section is about discovering and then cultivating that inner field, a secret preliminary action that sets the stage for our practice of meditation.

In Buddhism, *sila*, or moral conduct, always comes before *samadhi*, or strong meditation. In other words, the proper field for meditation is good behavior. From that foundation of basic goodness comes good meditation, and from that comes good lucid dreams. This is where we need to understand the subtle but important difference between mindfulness and attention. You can be attentive when you're aiming a gun to shoot someone, but you can't be mindful, because real mindfulness is a wholesome mental state. Associating true mindfulness with lucidity therefore implies that lucidity itself is at least partly dependent on morality.

In the world of dream yoga, which again is when lucid dreaming is used for spiritual practice, these tenets are unequivocal. If you want to be successful in dream yoga, you have to engage in good conduct. Lucid dreaming, on the other hand, is less strict, which is good news for those who aren't interested in using their dreams for spiritual practice. You can be a successful lucid dreamer and indulge your desires in your dreams, but that success will be driven by a different set of practices.

If these dream yoga tenets seem too religious for you, throw them out the window. I'm not passing judgment on anyone's aspirations for attaining lucidity. I still enjoy a romping fun time in my dreams, a "night out" with my fantasies. I'm simply trying to point out some of the more refined Eastern methods, and the spiritual principles upon which they are built.

EXERCISE: Checking In

Pause for a moment and journal how this preliminary practice settles with you. Does it resonate with you, and are you willing to abide by these tighter tenets?

_____

_____

_____

Or is it too self-righteous? The moniker for dream yoga in the ancient meditation texts is "the measure of the path." Do you take offense at being "measured" in this way? Explain your response.

_____

_____

_____

_____

If you chafe at these constraints, feel free to skip these methods. Like all of the techniques covered in this book, they're not for everyone. But spiritual practices can be powerful if they resonate with you.

MAGIC INDUCTION METHODS

The following Eastern techniques are "magic methods" of induction. I refer to them this way because their effects are indeed magical—if you believe in them. See how they settle with you.

Compassion

The meditation master Khenpo Rinpoche says that it is difficult to accelerate progress on the spiritual path. Things have to unfold in their own way. He then says, however, that there is one thing that can facilitate this path: walking it for the benefit of others. This takes the idea of moral conduct a notch higher and makes the field of dreams even more fertile. With this approach, you're not merely trying to stay out of trouble, or to engage in basic moral behavior. You're now acting with the primary intent to be of benefit to others. You're going to practice lucid dreaming with the heartfelt motivation to help this world. If this compassion method sounds appealing to you, try the following practice.

EXERCISE: Dedicated Intent

When you lie down to go to sleep tonight, put your hands over your heart and say something like, "May I attain lucidity in my sleep tonight so that I can better guide others to lucidity in their dreams and in their lives." The exact words don't really matter; it's the intention that matters. Make up your own bedtime aspiration and deliver it from your heart. If you are so moved, you can also make a dedication when you wake up in the morning. Whether or not you had any lucid dreams, say something like, "I dedicate the merit of my sleep and dreams last night to all sentient beings." (Merit in Buddhism is virtually synonymous with good actions, or good karma.) In this way you can sandwich your sleep with a sacred pre and post intent. Write both dedications here.

Evening Dedication: _____

_____

Morning Dedication: _____

_____

How does this first magic method settle with you?

_____

_____

_____

Devotion

The second magic method is devotion, or the power of prayer. In the *bhakti yoga* tradition of Hinduism, devotional Christianity, or *guru yoga* in Buddhism, devotion is everything. The idea is to open your heart and call upon powers greater than yourself for help. It's a mystical or supernatural approach that has a strong basis in many wisdom traditions. Cry out from the bottom of your heart to any spiritual being you have a connection with or already worship. It works the same magical way that blessings work. Dream yoga masters sometimes recommend that, as you place your head on your pillow, you imagine you're placing it in the lap of your spiritual teacher.

Some wisdom traditions have special dream deities, with prayers and mantras devoted to them. In the Bön tradition, practitioners supplicate the protector and guardian of sacred sleep, Salgye Du Dalma ("she who clarifies beyond conception"). Shamans often rely on spirit guides in the dream world, and Carl Jung had his dream assistant, Philemon, of which he said, "Philemon and other figures of my fantasies brought home to me the crucial insight that there are things in the psyche which I do not produce, but which produce themselves and have their own life. Philemon represented a force that was not myself."[33] With these magical methods of compassion, devotion, and the dedication of merit, you're using the laws of proximate karma, opening your heart to magic and mystery, and sanctifying your sleep.

EXERCISE: Prayer of Intent

Write a devotional prayer here. If the idea of prayer doesn't resonate with you, consider it an intention, or describe your own personal dream assistant that you'd like to see in your dream world. If this passage speaks to you, then memorize it and recite it every night as you go to bed. Use your imagination, your intuition, and your good heart to create your own sleep prayer.

_____

_____

_____

_____

_____

_____

Now look back and read this prayer or intention. Does it help you create a sacred space for your sleep? Is this something that feels right for you to do, or does it feel too religious? Write your thoughts here.

_____

_____

_____

_____

_____

_____

QUESTIONS AND ANSWERS

Doesn't the practice of illusory form, saying "This is a dream," contradict the practice of conducting state checks? I thought we wanted to confirm that we're not dreaming when we conduct a state check.

These are two different practices with similar *relative* goals (attaining lucidity in your dreams) but different *absolute* goals (assessing the nature of reality altogether). In the world of lucid dreaming, when you conduct a state check and confirm that you're not dreaming, that is considered as awake as you can get. Not so in the world of dream yoga. In dream yoga, a state check confirms that you're not dreaming in the Western sense, but you're probably still dreaming in the Eastern sense. In other words, in the Eastern view, just because you're not in the nighttime dream—what they call the "example dream" or "double delusion"—does not mean you're not still stuck in the "real dream" or "primary delusion" of waking life. It's a subtle but profound point that further distinguishes lucid dreaming from dream yoga. In the world of dream yoga, if a state check confirms you're not in the nighttime dream, but you still perceive waking reality in a dualistic way, you're still dreaming in the spiritual sense. You're still caught up and swept away by the contents of the real dream, or primary delusion. Waking up from that dream (the dream of daily life) is the *big* awakening, real lucidity, and the deeper purpose of dream yoga. Dream yoga takes the insights of waking up to your nighttime dreams and extrapolates them to help you wake up *to*—and then *from*—your daytime dream. That's absolute lucidity, or the awakening of the buddhas.

The practice of illusory form sounds like it rides on the practice of mindfulness. Is that an accurate way to look at it?

Yes. It's actually a form of mindfulness in disguise or another instance of stealth help. The practice of illusory form rides on the coattails of mindfulness, in that you first bring your mind back to what's happening (the mindfulness part) and then add to that the recognition of the maxim "This is a dream" (the illusory form part). It's another "twofer" practice; you're getting two benefits for the price of one.

I'm getting into lucid dreaming, but my sleeping partner is not. I don't see any way I can turn my bedroom into a temple, or do some of these techniques, without their thinking I'm crazy. What can I do?

This is a tricky one, and only you can really answer it. Every situation will be different. But the idea of the "middle way" can help. You have to respect your partner and not impose your newfound passion for lucidity upon them. Otherwise, you may well end up sleeping alone! But you also have to respect yourself and the value that these nocturnal practices are bringing to you. Tell your partner how much lucid dreaming means to you, and fully acknowledge that some of these techniques may appear strange. Bring a sense of self-effacing humor, which can often disarm others. But be genuine about it. This is another reason why I offer so many different methods. Some of them may work well for you and for those around you. Others may not. You don't want to turn a partner against you or have them disparage the practice of lucid dreaming. Maybe invite them to read part of this book that you feel is the most user-friendly. See if you can gently invite them into your brave new world.

I like the idea of opening up to powers greater than myself, but I'm an atheist. I don't pray to anyone.

You don't need an anthropomorphic image of a deity, creator principle, or guide to receive grace or blessing. It's the opening that's important, not the training wheels that get you to open. It's like lucidity altogether: lucidity is the point, not the method that gets you there. Touch into your heart, and do what feels right for you in terms of allowing yourself to open. While I'm a student of Buddhism (adhering to the Zen adage, "Chase two rabbits, catch none"), no one has a patent on truth. Wisdom has no form, but it takes on form because we believe in form. Without something to relate to, some form or image, it's hard for most of us to open up, surrender (in the good way), or otherwise release our grip on our limited sense of self. For agnostics, atheists, nontheists, and the like, these "magic methods" simply may not be for you. That's perfectly fine.

CHAPTER 8

Western Nighttime
Induction Techniques

As darkness descends, we begin our transition into the nighttime methods for inducing lucidity. The day may be closing, but the night is just opening. The natural curfew of the night restricts outward-bound activity but invites inward-bound adventures. With the techniques in the next two chapters, we're going to take full advantage of this grand opening by constructing an off-ramp from the speediness of life, while simultaneously building an on-ramp into lucidity. This will allow us to gently coast into the dream world with a new sense of awareness.

I recommend giving each technique a chance to work, at least a few weeks or even a month. If you see no progress, don't get discouraged. Write what you've experienced, and try something else. If you track your hits and misses, you'll start to discover patterns. You'll slowly see things you've never seen about yourself. That in itself is a practice of lucidity, or awareness, that can mature into lucid dreams.

SLEEP HYGIENE

The first general nighttime induction method is to practice good sleep hygiene. Most of us go to sleep "dirty," with a mind soiled by a sloppy attitude toward our dreams and stained by the stress of the day. Does this describe your general attitude to sleep? Or do you already respect sleep and dreams more?

_____

_____

If you went for a sweaty run at the end of the day, you probably wouldn't plop into bed before taking a shower. Similarly, you don't want to drop into sleep with a mucky mind. You want to approach the night with more respect.

In ancient Greece, lavish temples were devoted to Asclepius, the god of medicine and healing. In an effort to receive a curative dream from the Divine Physician, supplicants would engage in fasting, ritual purification, offerings, meditations, and a host of other preparatory practices that created a sacred space for dreaming. The dreams would then be interpreted by temple "translators" and used to heal the supplicant. Asclepius had five daughters, one of whom was Hygieia, the goddess of hygiene and sanitation. So we turn to the spirit of Hygieia to clean up our nighttime act and create our own temple of sleep.

The following are established methods for good sleep hygiene. We area all different. We can each build our temple in a personal way.

Before you read the following tips, write down your own ideas for how to improve your relationship to sleep.

_____

_____

_____

One caveat about this advice: There are no hard-and-fast rules with sleep hygiene, so your mileage may definitely vary. But for most of us, these all will help support good sleep.

Avoid Stimulants Close to Bedtime

Caffeine is one of the most traded commodities on earth, second only to oil. It is also the most widely used psychopharmaceutical stimulant on the planet. Caffeine is the only addictive substance we freely offer to children and adolescents. It is found in more places than you might think: dark chocolate, ice cream, pain relievers, weight-loss pills, and of course energy drinks and tea. *Decaffeinated* does not mean *noncaffeinated*. A cup of decaf coffee has 15 to 30 percent of the dose of a regular cup of coffee. Do you consume any of these products? Is it reasonable for you to cut back?

_____

_____

For good sleep, stop consuming caffeine around noon. Caffeine has a half-life of five to seven hours, which means that if you drink coffee at noon, 50 percent of the caffeine is still in your system from five to seven o'clock. Some people can drink a pint of espresso just before bed and sleep like a baby (because they have a stronger version of the liver enzyme cytochrome, which metabolizes caffeine). Others can have a cup of coffee in the morning and be buzzed ten hours later. The older we get, the more sensitive we tend to become to caffeine, and the longer it takes for our body to clear it from our system.

Avoid Too Much Alcohol

Alcohol can accelerate the onset of sleep but rebound to make us restless later. Alcohol is one of the most potent suppressors of REM sleep, the phase in which we dream the most. When babies drink milk that is laced with alcohol (alcohol is readily absorbed in a mother's milk), their sleep is more disjointed, and they suffer a 20 to 30 percent suppression of REM sleep shortly thereafter. Alcohol consumption is often connected with nicotine use, and some people report that nicotine patches can enhance the clarity of their dreams. (Others even report it helps them with lucidity—but note that nicotine can also interfere with sleep.) Have you noticed the effects on your sleep and dreams when you drink?

_____

_____

Avoid a Big Meal Before Bed

Having a full stomach might help you get sleepy, but it can make you restless in bed. If you have to eat just before going to bed, do so in moderation. Have you noticed how a big meal affects your sleep and dreams? What happens if you go to sleep on an empty stomach?

_____

_____

Avoid Exercising Too Late

Exercise promotes good sleep, but not if it's too close to bedtime. Get your workout in at least three hours prior to sleep. There are people who can hit the gym late in the evening and still sleep like a baby. Does this describe you? What's been your experience with exercising just before bed?

_____

_____

Stick to a Routine

Train your body and mind by going to sleep and getting up at the same time each day, plus or minus about twenty minutes. Avoid taking naps longer than thirty minutes during the day. Naps are great, but if you're too rested before bedtime it can interfere with the quality of your nighttime sleep by reducing *sleep pressure*. This natural, normal pressure is caused by the buildup of a chemical in your brain called *adenosine*, whose concentration increases with every waking minute. Caffeine dampens the effects of adenosine temporarily, but it continues to build up, like water being held back by a dam. When the caffeine wears off and the dam breaks, the accumulated buildup of adenosine rushes in as the "caffeine crash," with the onset of overwhelming sleepiness.

Do you find yourself all over the map when it comes to sleeping times? Is it workable for you to regulate your schedule to go to sleep and wake up at the same time every day? What would you need to do to make this happen?

_____

_____

Don't Multitask in Bed

To create a healthy association between your bed and sleep, use it only for sleep and intimacy. Associations are powerful. If you start doing other business in bed, you will associate your bed with business. However, creating a pure atmosphere around sleep doesn't mean becoming puritanical. If you love to read in bed or engage in some other presleep ritual, and these help you drift off to sleep, use your judgment.

Keep Your Room Cool, Dark, and Quiet

Darkness releases melatonin, the "Dracula hormone" that only comes out at night to regulate good sleep. Melatonin supplements are best for jet lag, when you want to reset your internal clock. They're not that helpful as general sleep aids. If there's too much light, wear a sleep mask to keep things dark. Make sure your room is cool; around 66°F is the sweet spot. And keep your sleeping space quiet. If necessary, use earplugs or the sound of a fan or other white noise machine.

Power Down

Pull yourself away from computers, tablets, and smartphones two to three hours before sleep. Natural light sets our internal clock, but artificial light upsets it. The blue-light display of these electronic devices mimics daylight and suppresses the release of melatonin. Some ganglion cells in the brain have blue-light-sensitive receptors that tell our brain to set our circadian clock to night or day. The brighter and bluer the light, the more it affects these receptors and suppresses melatonin, especially when we're exposed to it up close and at night. Studies have shown that the sleep delay from exposure to the blue light from a tablet is some 96 minutes, for a smartphone it's 67 minutes, and for an e-reader with backlit display it's 58 minutes.

If you work late into the night or have a hard time putting your devices aside, consider wearing blue-light-blocking glasses or getting an app that filters the blue wavelength. If you're hard-core into sleep hygiene, create your own "red light district" by using dim red light for your night-lights. Red light has the least power to suppress melatonin and shift circadian rhythm.

Is your smartphone or tablet a regular sleeping partner? Do you feel you must have your gadgets within reach at all times? If so, you could benefit from some electronic detox. What changes could you make to give yourself a breather from constant connection?

_____

_____

_____

_____

Get Enough Sunshine

A regular daily dose of sunshine can help you sleep better by keeping you in tune with circadian rhythms. The brain relies on the sun to recognize the time for being awake and alert, which is another reason to curb light as you prepare for sleep. But too much sunshine can mess with sleep. When I was in Alaska around the summer solstice, it never really got dark. I became somewhat manic, high on all the light that kept me up at night.

EXERCISE: Strategy for Better Sleep

Which, if any, of these sleep hygiene strategies are you already using? Do you notice benefits already?

_____

_____

_____

Now pick at least one strategy that you aren't using, and consider how it might improve your sleep hygiene. How will you implement this change? Will it be easy or difficult? Is anything holding you back?

_____

_____

_____

_____

Are there any other strategies that you might want to try? Note that the benefits of these strategies will compound, so the more you implement, the more benefits you'll see.

_____

_____

LUCID SLEEP ONSET

The care and attention you bring to your sleep by properly preparing your bed with good sleep hygiene is part of lucid sleep onset. This includes everything you do just before going to bed, as well as the induction methods you do while you're lying in bed. It's another instance of the preliminaries being more important than the main practice. Every daytime technique already presented can slot into good lucid sleep onset if you engage in it just before you go to sleep. This includes meditating before sleep, resetting your strong intention to become lucid, the magic methods of compassion and devotion, and so on. For most people it's a complete revamping of how they normally fall asleep. Most of us just collapse into bed, zone out, or otherwise crash at the end of the day, succumbing to the power of our "dirty" non-lucid habits. Because of the laws of causality and proximate karma, this contributes to zoned-out, non-lucid dreams.

Encouraging lucid sleep onset is about creating a new bridge between day and night. It replaces that collapse with construction, zoning out with tuning in, crashing with building, falling into sleep with rising up into lucidity, and blacking out with lighting up. We may be "checking out" of daytime consciousness, but now we want to "check in" to nighttime awareness. That requires a paradigm shift and a retooling of our relationship to sleep and dreaming. Traditionally, sleep and dreaming are defined by a lack of awareness, so making this transition with lucidity goes against the grain of how we've been taught to fall asleep.

EXERCISE: Assessing Nighttime Induction Methods

As you start to implement these nighttime induction techniques, notice your relationship to them. Do you feel excited about trying these new approaches to sleep, or feel resistance, or something else?

_____

_____

Don't judge yourself; just observe your reactions to these techniques. Is there a point where these methods cross a line and you say to yourself, *Not for me?*

_____

_____

These nighttime induction methods will reveal the "forces of the dark side," all the shady habitual patterns we've spent our entire lives accumulating every night as we just crash non-lucidly into sleep. The force of these habits is exposed when we try to counteract them with our lucid sleep onset practices.

Look back on these journal entries as you continue with your lucid dreaming practice, and see how these reactions change as time goes on. After several weeks, has your enthusiasm—or resistance—changed, or do you have any new impressions?

_____

_____

_____

_____

_____

Countdown to Blast-Off

One of the simplest transitional practices is to count yourself down into sleep. You're now lying in bed. You've reset your intention to become lucid and, if you practice prayer, made your bedtime prayer for lucidity. Now you want to counteract the usually "too loose" attitude of collapsing into sleep with a practice that initially may seem a bit tight. But without this structure you're more likely to fall into sleep non-lucidly.

EXERCISE: Counting Down to Lucid Sleep

As you lie in bed, say to yourself mentally, *One, I'm dreaming...two, I'm dreaming...three, I'm dreaming...* Do this mindfully and slowly. You want to be focused as you begin to count down, and then gradually to release your grip. If you bounce to the other extreme and become too tight, you'll end up counting the entire night. You have to be flexible; play around with this technique and find your own way. Some nights you'll only get to ten before you slip into sleep; other nights you might count to a hundred. If you find yourself getting to a hundred, just drop it. The technique can backfire and stress you out—*I should be sleeping by now!*

This is a sly form of mindfulness meditation designed to sneak in some lucidity in your descent into sleep. The next morning, write down what you remember about how the technique worked. For example, you might have found yourself dipping into sleep and briefly popping up to return to your counting. Did the counting help you maintain a thread of awareness, or was it irritating and too intrusive?

_____

_____

If you hit the sweet spot in the countdown technique, you will find that at a certain number you really are dreaming, and chances are you're doing so lucidly. When that happens, journal your experience here. And be sure to date it.

_____

_____

_____

_____

_____

_____

_____

There are many variations of this kind of "decrescendo" technique, which is essentially performing a repetitive mental task in a relaxed but attentive way. You can count the proverbial sheep if you like. The idea is that you want to sustain lucidity as you go from "out loud" waking consciousness to the silence of sleep. Mentally "whispering" the countdown helps with this delicate transition.

The WILD and DILD Techniques

There are essentially two ways to attain lucidity in your dreams. One way is to bring awareness with you as you descend from the waking state into your dreams, what Stephen LaBerge calls a "wake-initiated lucid dream" (WILD). The countdown technique is a WILD technique. Your body falls asleep but your mind remains lucid or awake. We tend to think of sleep as mostly an on-off process, as represented in a normal light switch. One moment we're awake and consciousness is still lit up; a moment later we're asleep, and consciousness has turned off. The counting technique and other WILD methods replace the light switch with a dimmer. You're keeping a sliver of awareness on as you drop into sleep.

Most WILD dreams occur later in the evening when we're in REM sleep, or during afternoon naps. It's not easy to carry awareness directly into sleep when we first lie down, but the countdown practice greases the skids.

EXERCISE: **WILD Timing**

One of the best ways to engage WILD dreams is during the hypnagogic and hypnopompic phases, those transitional stages going into and emerging from sleep. The next time you go to sleep, try to pay attention to how thoughts slowly transition into images, how flashes of light and geometric patterns may appear, and how the images eventually morph into dreamlets. This half-dream state is a great place to go WILD, to explore being half awake and half asleep.

Can you sustain awareness here? What do you notice in the half-dream state? As soon as you're able, write down what you experience, even if you didn't see anything at first.

_____

_____

If you can remember a specific half-dream state from the past, describe it in as much detail as you recall. I'll describe one of my experiences in a half-dream state to help get you started:

Just last night I went to sleep thinking about the new car I want to buy. As I dozed off, the thought of the car gradually dissolved and was replaced by images of the car. I'd briefly pop back up into waking consciousness and start thinking about the car again, then drop back down where there were only images and no thoughts. Then I noticed how the images of the car began "inflating" into dreamlets, lasting just a few seconds. These would be of me now driving in the car, or washing it, or showing it off. I was totally aware that these were dreams, albeit short ones, so this awareness made these dreamlets lucid dreamlets. With practice, I have learned how to stay with the dreamlets and watch them further inflate into full-blown lucid dreams—like me racing my car along the French Riviera for miles on end, or even launching into the air!

Now it's your turn. Describe the half-dream state you experienced:

_____

_____

_____

_____

_____

_____

_____

_____

The second way to trigger a lucid dream is to initiate lucidity within a dream: a dream-initiated lucid dream, or DILD. You attain lucidity after you've fallen asleep in the usual unconscious way. Something *within* the dream clues you into the fact that you're dreaming. Dreamsigns and state checks, which we have already covered, are DILD techniques; we began with these techniques because DILDs are generally more frequent than WILDs.

To sum up, you either bring awareness with you as you fall asleep (WILD techniques) or trigger awareness within the dream when you're already asleep (DILD techniques). The result is the same: a lucid dream.

EXERCISE: **DILD Timing**

You may have some experience with DILDs already. If so, describe what you recall:

_____

_____

_____

_____

The MILD Technique

LaBerge devised a highly effective technique he called the "mnemonic induction of lucid dreams" (MILD). You've probably heard of a mnemonic device as a way to remember something; "mnemonic" just means an aid to memory. The acronyms WILD, DILD, and MILD, for instance, are themselves mnemonic devices. They're a lot easier to remember than "wake-initiated lucid dream," "dream-initiated lucid dream," and "mnemonic induction of lucid dreams," respectively. MILD dreams work the same way. They employ prospective memory that is used after you wake up from a dream at night and before you fall back asleep. (Don't confuse the acronym MILD with the quality of being "mild"—it's just an acronym.) Here are the four steps of MILD:

1. Early in the morning, or when you awaken spontaneously from a dream during the night, go over the dream several times until you have memorized it. Hit the rewind button in your mind and play it back a few times until it stays with you.

2. Then, while lying in bed and returning to sleep, say to yourself several times, *The next time I'm dreaming, I will remember to recognize I'm dreaming.* Reset your intention to become lucid.

3. Visualize yourself as being back in the dream you just rehearsed, only this time see yourself realizing that you are in fact dreaming. Imagine that you're back in the dream, but now fully lucid to it.

4. Repeat steps 2 and 3 until you feel your intention is clearly fixed or you fall back to sleep.

It takes practice to make the MILD technique second nature, but with time you will find yourself automatically defaulting into it when you wake up during the night, or after any dream. Let's try a dry run.

EXERCISE: **Recall and Rehearse**

1. Describe the last dream you can remember, in as much detail as you can recall. Or, if you can't remember a dream right now, come back to this activity as soon as you wake up tomorrow morning.

_____

_____

_____

_____

2. Repeat this dream to yourself, over and over. This will help you remember it so that you can recall the dream later when you're in bed.

3. Visualize yourself as being back in the dream you just rehearsed, only this time see yourself realizing that you are in fact dreaming. Imagine that you're back in the dream, but now fully lucid to it.

4. Repeat steps 2 and 3 before bed. Do so until either you feel your intention is clearly fixed or you fall back asleep.

Journal about your experience below.

_____

_____

_____

_____

Wake-and-Back-to-Bed Technique

The wake-and-back-to-bed method is said to increase your chances of lucidity by up to 1,600 percent, a sixteen-fold increase. Because my own experience supports this data, this is my go-to method.

Before we explore the technique: have you ever noticed any difference in your dreams when you get up later in the night to go to the bathroom (or whatever) and then go back to sleep? If so, describe the difference:

_____

_____

_____

EXERCISE: Wake-and-Back-to-Bed

Set your alarm to go off two to three hours before you would normally wake up. You may have to tweak the timing, either getting up a bit earlier or a bit later, but with experimentation you will discover your sweet zone.

When the alarm goes off, stay up for twenty to forty minutes, a range of time you can adjust depending on your own sleep patterns. (With lots of practice, I now need to stay up for only a few minutes for this method to work, so I frequently use it when I have to get up in the night to go to the bathroom.) During your initial twenty to forty minutes, reset your intention to have lucid dreams, meditate, or do some light reading about lucid dreaming, then go back to sleep. Do *not* check your phone, or go to your tablet or computer. Stay away from excessive light and refrain from activity. You don't want to overly engage your waking consciousness, which can yank you out of the sleep state for the rest of the night.

After you try the wake-and-back-to-bed technique, journal your experience upon awakening:

_____

_____

_____

Track what works and doesn't work for you. If you got up three hours before normal waking, did the back-to-bed technique, and nothing happened, journal that. It's not a failure. Your efforts to log that data will help you adjust the technique. It's like tuning in a radio station until the frequency is just right.

EXERCISE: **Strategy to Customize Your Wake-and-Back-to-Bed**

Write out your plan for the wake-and-back-to-bed method.

Do you normally wake up to use the bathroom or will you set an alarm? At what time?

_____

_____

What will you do for twenty to forty minutes awake? Meditate? Read? If so, what? Remember not to check your phone or look at your tablet.

_____

_____

Remember to journal about your experience. Use the space here to get started; continue later on in your dream journal.

_____

_____

_____

_____

If you tried this technique and it feels awkward, or you find this technique doesn't speak to you, journal that.

_____

_____

_____

_____

_____

_____

This tracking is in the spirit of what scientists call "longitudinal studies," which means collecting data over extended periods. A good scientist reports any experimental finding, even if the experiment is a failure. Those failures allow them to refine their methods. In this way, as a good sleep scientist, you will discover patterns of what works and what doesn't work.

ELECTRIFY YOUR DREAMS

Are you someone who enjoys electronic gadgets? Here are some devices you can try. One of the most effective is a dream mask, originally conceived by LaBerge in 1985. The mask works in an ingenious way. Sensors inside the mask are designed to detect the eye movement that indicates the REM stage of sleep. A cue is delivered via gentle flashing lights or sound, which prompts the dreamer to become lucid. The cues enter your dream and become incorporated into it, similar to what happens when it gets cold in your bedroom and you find yourself dreaming about snow or ice. What's outside you affects what's inside you.

Have you had the experience of outside stimuli, like temperature, sounds, smells, or tactile sensations, influencing your dreams? Starting today, pay attention to how external circumstances influence your internal states when you sleep, and jot down those influences here.

_____

_____

When I wear the mask, I often dream of waiting in my dream car at a stoplight and then wondering why the light is blinking. I'll suddenly remember to connect the flashing light in my dream with the blinking light in the mask, and I'm instantly lucid. In variations, a flashing streetlight will clue me in, or the pumping of brake lights in a car in front of me.

There are also sleep-monitoring devices (such as Sleeptracker, Basis Peak - Ultimate Fitness and Sleep Tracker, Neuroon Open, and Aurora Dreamband) for those who are interested in a detailed analysis of sleep cycles. These can tell you how many times a night you drop into REM sleep by measuring and recording a number of biosignals via electroencephalogram (EEG), electromyography (EMG), and electrooculography (EOG), which measure brain waves, muscle tension, and eye movement, respectively. These mini sleep labs are for the deep diver; they can help you refine your awareness of sleep patterns, or what scientists call "sleep architecture."

Finally, a number of lucid dreaming apps are available for your smartphone, including DreamZ, Lucid Dreamer, Lucidity, and Awoken. These apps offer functions like reality checkers, alarms, binaural beats, and other features to help you record and study your dreams. And for the sexually adventurous reader, Dream Rooster is a "sex dream machine" that claims to stimulate not only lucid dreaming but also other parts of your body-mind matrix.

HERBAL SUPPLEMENTS

For those interested in the use of herbs, a host of supplements are available. The only one that I have used with consistent success is galantamine. Galantamine is extracted from the snowdrop (*Galanthus nivalis*) and spider lily plants (*Lycoris* species) and is used to enhance memory and delay the onset of memory disorders. Studies have shown that this nootropic (cognitive enhancer) is effective for many people in inducing lucidity.[34]

Galantamine works by inhibiting the breakdown of the neurotransmitter acetylcholine, which is found to be in high concentration when you're dreaming. Galantamine increases both the duration and the level of action of this neurotransmitter, which tends to make dreams longer and clearer, giving you a better chance at recognition. You can start with 4 milligrams, taken either in the middle of the night or before that two- to three-hour prime dreamtime window before you wake up. If nothing happens, try 8 milligrams. To prevent tolerance, don't take it more than twice a week.

There are dozens of other herbs that I have not used, but that my dream colleagues endorse. If you're inclined to do some research, you can look into *Calea zacatechichi*, mugwort, kratom (*Mitragyna speciosa*), *Silene undulata*, *Banisteriopsis caapi*, valerian root, velvet bean, Syrian rue, iboga (*Tabernanthe iboga*), kava, yohimbe, salvia, skullcap, tart cherry, and blue lotus—to name a few.

Pay attention to your diet, and see if there are any patterns between what you eat and how you dream. Do the same thing for any medications you take. Just looking into these connections will help you refine your understanding of how you sleep and dream. Write down your discoveries here.

_____

_____

_____

_____

Here's a set of exercises that will help you cultivate the proper outlook for all the induction techniques.

EXERCISE: **The Comfort Zone**

Draw three concentric circles—a small central one, and two others encircling it.

At the center is your comfort zone, where you love to hang out and take it easy. It's your bubble bath mentality. Does this zone define you? How important is your comfort zone? Are you the happiest when you're in your bubble bath? Do you get irritated when something interrupts you in your cozy zone or cuts into your plan to just luxuriate? Write about this:

_____

_____

_____

_____

_____

The comfort zone is characterized by being too loose. This zone is fine, but not if that's the only place you want to stay. If you only hang out in your cozy bubble bath, you'll never grow. You'll eventually drown in comfort. If you spend too much time here, the comfort zone becomes the cemetery of the self. Personal evolution stops dead in its tracks.

Growth occurs when you stretch into the *challenge zone*, the second concentric circle. To stretch into lucidity, you need to reach outside your comfort zone. This is not always comfortable, because when it comes to falling asleep the force of habit is formidable, and our comfort plans are unyielding. For many people, falling into blissful sleep each night is akin to plopping into a mental bubble bath. Who wants to challenge that?

Lucid dreaming, and especially dream yoga, are forms of mental yoga. They are designed to stretch your mind into previously unconscious states—and out of your comfort zone.

EXERCISE: The Challenge Zone

How willing are you to be stretched? Does stretching stimulate you or intimidate you? Write about this:

_____

_____

_____

_____

_____

_____

_____

The final circle is the *danger zone* or *risk zone*. You're in this zone when you've gone too far, overextending the stretch into a *snap* by trying too hard. That's being too tight. In terms of lucid dreaming, this zone is where you try so hard that you keep yourself up, tying yourself in knots in your efforts to get lucid. Growth usually doesn't happen at this outer limit, although you can learn from your excesses. The risk zone is where people get bruised or otherwise ding themselves through overexertion. In the world of lucid dreaming, this is often the point where people drop out.

EXERCISE: Danger, Comfort, or Challenge?

How do you feel about thrill seeking? Perhaps you like living on the edge, or even going over it now and again. Or maybe the "outer limits" frighten you. Write about this:

_____

_____

_____

_____

If your goal is to live in the comfort zone, you will discover that it gets smaller and smaller, and the effort required to become lucid just isn't worth it. You prefer to snooze and capitulate to your comfort plans, as represented by security blankets like your comforter. As we age, we tend to default more to our comfort zone and get fussier about exactly what that is. We get more territorial, consciously or unconsciously defending our comfort zone.

Have you noticed this? Do you complain more than you did when you were younger? Do you find yourself developing the mentality *I can't be bothered*? These could be signs that your comfort zone is shrinking. Describe your changed responses and feelings:

_____

_____

_____

_____

However, if you make the effort and stretch yourself into the challenge zone, you'll find your comfort zone expanding. You'll complain less and tolerate more. You'll be more willing to inconvenience your normal sleep habits and to make the effort to "wake up."

So for this exercise, be honest with yourself and journal about times when you feel yourself being stretched into the challenge zone, or when you overextend into the danger zone. Do some of these techniques reach too far? If so, write about this.

_____

_____

_____

It's like yoga: are you willing to tolerate the necessary and healthy stretch? Write down why you're willing to tolerate the stretch—or why not.

_____

_____

_____

Remember, we're trying to expand consciousness from the day into the night, so the ability to tolerate stretching is helpful. Some people are okay with the daytime techniques but draw the line with nighttime methods. "You can rouse me during the day, but leave me alone when I sleep!" That's okay. Then just stick with the daytime techniques.

If you find yourself saying, *Maybe lucid dreaming isn't for me after all*, or *This is going too far*, recognize that you may be feeling stretched to the snapping point, and back off. Return to your bubble bath. Give yourself a break. Then step out of the tub again for another try.

Use these exercises to learn about yourself, not to judge or criticize yourself. Dreams are truth tellers, and working with lucid dreaming is similarly truth telling. Be truthful when you do this exercise, and perhaps you'll discover that it's not just lucid dreaming that is enclosed by these three circles, but your entire life. Do these concentric circles—comfort, challenge, and danger—apply to other aspects of your life? Write down some areas where they do:

_____

_____

_____

QUESTIONS AND ANSWERS

I like the idea of the dream mask, but I can't afford it. Is there any other way to achieve this dream stimulation?

Yes, if you have a willing partner. In the traditional dream yoga texts, a dream yogi would have a partner at their side as they fell asleep. The awake partner would watch the sleeping partner, and when they felt they were asleep they would whisper things like, "You're dreaming now; wake up to your dream." With your understanding of sleep cycles and REM sleep, you can target the dreaming state more specifically than the yogis of old. In other words, if you have a willing partner, they can wait until they see your eyes darting around under closed lids, or notice the muscle twitches associated with REM sleep, and then whisper in your ear. You could also set a timer to initiate the playback of a recording some ninety minutes after you fall asleep, when you're in your first REM cycle. Once you get the basic principles, you can get creative and come up with all kinds of tricks.

I've heard that sensory deprivation can help trigger lucid dreams—is this true?

There is some preliminary data on this and lots of anecdotal evidence. Some people swear that flotation tanks work to induce lucidity. I've tried it; I loved soaking in the warm salt water, but I didn't have any luck with lucid dreaming. I have had consistent success spending time in total darkness. This is not for everyone, partly because spending days in a pitch-black room is more difficult than flotation tanks, and many people really are afraid of the dark. It's not easy to find pitch-black rooms, or extended periods of time to spend in them. But for the intrepid explorers out there, sensory deprivation is an option.

Does sleeping with a soft light on, or any other source of illumination, help trigger lucid dreams?

It can. The idea is that external light is not the same as the light of the mind, but it's also not different. You can therefore use outside light to invoke inside light, so to speak. Remember, a lucid dream is a "lit or illuminated dream": a dream in which the light of awareness (or *meta-awareness*, awareness of awareness) has been turned on, and you see things never seen before. With an external light filtering into your sleep, the theory goes, you can more readily see that the dream is indeed a dream. Again, it's akin to how a cold room can trigger dreams of snow or ice. Something gets through to the dreaming mind.

Here's a contemplation to help with this radical notion of internal light. When you view your dreams, lucid or not, what illuminates the objects in your dream? There's no sun or other light source in there, but we still "see" the objects in our dreams. Where does that light come from? It comes from the light of the mind itself.

CHAPTER 9

Eastern Nighttime Induction Techniques

This chapter is a deeper dive into the nuances of Eastern approaches to lucidity. These techniques have been enormously effective on my own path, and for countless others, but they may not be for everybody. We're all different. Be your own guide, and do what feels right for you. If this approach doesn't resonate with you, feel free to move on to Part III: What to Do with Lucid Dreams.

Like the Western methods, the Eastern nighttime methods also begin with good sleep hygiene. Recall that sleep is a variable mental factor—either positive, negative, or neutral, depending on the immediately preceding state of mind. We want to make sleep positive and "clean" using the following techniques, conjoined with the laws of karma/habit as discussed earlier. Once we set our pure intention for lucidity, sprinkled with the magic ingredients of compassion and devotion, we can turn to specific Eastern nighttime techniques.

Eastern versions of sleep hygiene begin with the cleansing power of meditation. Settle your mind with an evening meditation session. I meditate for at least thirty minutes every night before bed, a ritual as regular as brushing my teeth. It's like brushing my mind, freeing it from the debris gathered during the day. If you can manage only a few minutes of meditation prior to sleep, that will help.

Write down how you usually feel before going to bed. Is your mind speedy from the day? Are you stressed, worried, or otherwise "soiled"?

Now sit and meditate for a few minutes. Write down how that makes you feel. Does meditation reveal how speedy your mind actually is? Does it help your mind settle down?

_____

_____

_____

_____

In this busy age, we're human "doings" more than we're human beings. Falling asleep requires that we become "undone"—that we fully let go of the day and *fall* into sleep. Sleeping should be the easiest and most natural thing for human beings to do, yet many human doings struggle to let go of the doing at bedtime. We have to do nothing—but we have to do it well. Not so easy for human doings. This is where meditation fits in, because "doing nothing well" is one definition of meditation.

Here are some other reasons why meditation is so helpful just before bed.

THE SUBTLE BODY

Many of the induction methods from the East rely on the inner subtle body. We're familiar with the gross outer body, its remarkable anatomy and physiology, and the popular outer yoga practices that work with it. The outer body includes our brain, which supports gross waking consciousness. But many of us are unacquainted with the subtle inner body, which has its own anatomy and physiology, as well as lesser-known inner yoga forms that work with it. The subtle inner body includes processes that support subtle dreaming consciousness.

According to Eastern thought, the outer body is an expression of the inner body. We can subdivide the subtle body into many classes, including the energy body, emotional body, astral body, celestial body, etheric body, and mental body. Eastern medical systems target this subtle body for healing; Eastern mysticism targets this same body for spiritual transformation. In the tantric traditions, the body is as important as the mind. The outer and inner yoga practices work with both the gross and the subtle body, as a way to work with both the gross and the subtle mind. What kind of relationship do you have to your body? Do you appreciate it? Or do you find it a nuisance? Does your body get in the way of your spiritual practice?

_____

_____

_____

Have you ever tried yoga? If not, why not?

_____

_____

We're always working with the two-way street between body and mind, gross and subtle, whether we know it or not. Psychosomatic illnesses are one illustration of how gross states of mind—like stress—can adversely affect our physical body. Conversely, positive states of mind have been shown to positively affect the body. So this "interstate commerce" is already happening between mind and body. With both outer and inner yoga, we want to direct this import-export business to achieve the profits of lucidity.

Dream yoga is an inner yoga, which means it engages the subtle body to invoke subtle (dream level) states of mind. Using the tenets of bidirectionality, by becoming more aware of your subtle body, you will find yourself becoming more lucid to the dream state that is supported by this body. In other words, it's not just your mind that's non-lucid, but also your body. Working with outer and inner yoga "wakes up" the subtle body, which will then "wake you up" to your dreams.

We'll begin by briefly describing the anatomy and physiology of the subtle body, which means this introduction is cognitive. It's just a map. The real introduction takes place when you drop from your head into your body, when you literally *feel* your subtle body. With the exercises in this chapter we'll do precisely that. We'll drop the outer map and enter the inner territory.

You already feel the subtle body, but you may not know it. When you're touched by beautiful music, it's your subtle body that's being touched. I recently went to a concert of kirtan, the ancient devotional music of India that is sometimes called "the song of the Soul." After two hours of glorious chanting and singing, I left feeling like I had just bathed my subtle body, a feeling of openness and purity. The kirtan singer Ragani says, "Kirtan is a means of finding our way back to the core of our Being." As a classical pianist, I find that Beethoven, Schubert, and Chopin have that same power to move me. There is something primeval and transcendent about sound. (Even physicists talk about the fundamental nature of matter in terms of *string theory*, a suggestion that at physical levels the world rests on a bed of "sound.") The universe itself allegedly came into existence with a big bang.

The subtle body can't be seen with an X-ray or MRI, so there is no way to measure it using gross Western methods. But absence of this gross evidence is not evidence of the subtle body's absence. It's just that Western instruments aren't subtle enough. The subtle body is as real (or in Eastern philosophy, as *unreal*) as the outer body. If we don't take it too literally, the subtle body is made of "sound" and "light," which is why music touches it and mantra works with it. Even in Christianity it is taught: "In the beginning was the word, and the word was made flesh." In the beginning was the subtle inner, and it was made into gross outer.

A Sanskrit scholar at Banaras Hindu University once told me that in ancient Indian lore, someone who masters Sanskrit develops mastery over the phenomenal world. He argued that Sanskrit is the language of reality, which is one reason Sanskrit mantras are never translated. It's the actual sound, not the meaning, that delivers the impact. Such a linguistic master, a primordial "conductor" in resonance with reality, can allegedly affect the physical world with miraculous incantation.

EXERCISE: Tuning in to the Subtle Body

Let's contact this subtle body further. Take a break and listen to your favorite music—the most beautiful melodies you can find. Close your eyes and settle into your body. Does the sound reach you in your heart, or perhaps your gut? The subtle body *is* subtle. You have to really listen and feel within (and work with *interoception* and *proprioception*). Write down what you feel and where you feel it.

_____

_____

_____

_____

Once you tune in to the subtle body and become more familiar with it, you can start to fine-tune it with the exercises that follow.

The subtle body has a complex structure that is well beyond the scope of this book. For our purposes, we need to know only about four key features: the channels, winds, drops, and wheels; or in Sanskrit, *nadis, prana, bindus,* and *chakras,* respectively. Each of these subtle body features has gross body correlates, as we will see.

Channels and Winds

Let's start with the channels, which are the easiest to understand. Thousands of subtle channels (*meridians* in Chinese medicine) course through the subtle body, but we need to know about only three of them. The central channel runs from the top of the head to the base of the spine, and two side channels start at the nostrils, ascend up to the top of the head, and then descend parallel to the central channel down to the base of the spine. The outer body equivalents to the inner channels are the arteries, veins, and nervous system—anything that conducts life force energy.

These channels, or nadis, are not solid, fixed entities. Through inner yoga practices they can be altered, which in turn alters how the subtle winds flow through them, which alters how your mind works. We previously touched on the concept of neuroplasticity. Nadis work the same way, abiding by the tenets of *nadiplasticity*. By changing your mind you not only change your brain, you also change your nadis. And in the spirit of bidirectionality, by changing your nadis through inner yoga, you can also change your mind. We'll engage this principle in several of the following exercises.

Mantras work to straighten out the channels. If we could somehow take an X-ray of the subtle body, we would find a network of twisted and knotted channels, an actual physiology that supports the expressions of how stressful situations "tie us into knots" or make us feel "uptight" and "strung out." Reciting a mantra serves to iron out these channels (with different mantras targeting different channels); this allows the subtle winds to flow through them more gracefully, which invokes graceful states of mind.

Within these channels flow the subtle winds, or prana, also called *chi, qi, lung, Holy Spirit* in esoteric Christianity, and *Holy Wind* by the Navajo. "Wind" is such a big force that even the word "spirit" derives from a root that means "breath," which is our most intimate "wind." The outer body analog is respiration. Many yoga masters assert that yoga is fundamentally about working with these winds. In some of the highest tantras it is taught that wind is the most powerful force in the universe. The Kalachakra tantra, the "king of tantras," states that wind creates and destroys individual and collective world systems. In Shambhala Buddhism, the practice of *windhorse* is harnessed to create "enlightened society." If wind can do all that, then we can surely use it to harness lucid dreams.

EXERCISE: The Breath Connection

There is an intimate connection between your breath, the quality of your mind, and the movement of thought. Depressed people don't breathe deeply. A depressed patient once told me, "I have no space inside!"—perhaps because there was no wind to activate that sense of space. The next time you're angry or upset, notice your respiration and describe it here:

_____

_____

_____

The next time you feel any intense emotion, look at your breathing and journal what you see.

_____

_____

_____

_____

_____

_____

When you witness something breathtaking, notice how that experience can literally stop your breath, and therefore your mind. These invitations to look and feel within will help you tune in to your subtle body— and also serve to awaken it.

Now put this book down and meditate for ten minutes, noticing whether the velocity of your thoughts is related to the velocity of your breath. When your mind settles, does your breath settle? Journal what you notice.

_____

_____

_____

_____

_____

Seasoned meditators can enter a state of deep meditation in which breathing slows down dramatically and sometimes actually stops. These meditative absorptions (*samadhi*) are not uncommon; they occur when all thoughts cease. Some inner yoga practices (*tummo, khumbhaka, pranayama, lungta*) target respiration directly as a way to invoke subtle states of mind. And remember: dreams are made of mind, and mind rides these subtle winds. When harnessed properly, we can ride these winds into lucidity.

Drops and Wheels

The winds flow through the channels and carry the drops. These drops, or *bindus*, are perhaps the hardest of these concepts to understand. They are sometimes called *mind pearls*, and the best way to think of them is simply as "drops of consciousness." The inner yoga methods (and remember, lucid dreaming/dream yoga is an inner yoga) have a lot to say about these drops, but for our purposes this is all we need to know. Outer body correlates would be sperm, ovum, hormones, neurotransmitters, or any concentration of life force energy.

The final component is also the most famous, the wheels, or *chakras*. Chakras are energy distribution centers located along the body's central channel: base of the spine, genitals, solar plexus, heart, throat, forehead, and top of the head. Outer body equivalents are the endocrine centers: the adrenal glands, testes or ovaries, pancreas, thymus, thyroid, pituitary, and pineal glands, respectively. Depending on the system, each chakra is associated with a frequency or sound and color. We need to become familiar with only three chakras and their frequencies:

- The head chakra is white, and its sound is "OM."

- The throat chakra is red, and its sound is "AH."

- The heart chakra is blue, and its sound is "HUM."

Different traditions describe variations with the subtle body in terms of the sound and color of the chakras, but don't tie yourself into knots worrying about that.

EXERCISE: Resonating with the Chakras

Sit in meditation and close your eyes. Let your mind settle. Slowly chant OM for a few minutes. Subtle often means slow, so chant these syllables mindfully. Then journal what you feel and where you feel it.

Now chant AH over and over. Write down what you feel and where you feel it. If you don't feel a thing, write that down.

_____

_____

Now chant HUM repeatedly, and journal what you feel. Do these sounds and subtle feelings invite you in? Where do you feel them?

_____

_____

These exercises are subtle; they compel you to listen and feel intently. I am trying to introduce you to subtle dimensions of your being, which is where the dreaming mind abides. These inner yoga methods are slow and quiet, and for the fast and loud mind they might generate a response like, *I don't notice or feel a thing.* That's okay. Just be patient, and notice that as your mind gets quiet you can start to resonate with these subtle states. The more familiar you get with your subtle body/mind during the day, the more you'll be able to recognize it when you sleep and dream.

PUTTING IT ALL TOGETHER

The induction techniques that follow are based on this core principle: the states of consciousness that we experience in the waking, dreaming, and deep dreamless states are dictated by the operation of these four aspects of the subtle body: channels, winds, drops, and wheels. Right now you're awake, which means the drops are gathered in the head chakra. When you fall asleep, the drops literally fall from the head center into the heart center, which is the inner body correlate to deep dreamless sleep. This is why we sometimes jerk ourselves awake as consciousness literally drops into sleep. It is often felt as falling.

When you fall asleep tonight, pay attention to any sense of descent. When you wake up tomorrow, write down what you felt last night. If you didn't feel or notice a thing, write that down. Then try this exercise again tomorrow.

_____

_____

When you wake up, it's because the drops are literally being blown back up by the inner winds, which often is felt as an arising. The drops fly back up into your head and activate all the speediness of your busy and windy mind. Sometimes the arousal can be jarring, like when you're rudely woken up in the middle of the night. It's almost as if the bindus are slamming into the top of your head.

Write down what you notice when you first wake up. Is there a sense of ascent? Do you notice that thoughts are relatively still when you first get up and get increasingly "windy" as you move further into waking consciousness?

Waking *up* in the morning and settling *down* in the evening are linguistic equivalents of this subtle body process. Crashing, collapsing, plunging, sinking, plopping, keeling over, lapsing, and dipping into sleep are all synonyms of this nocturnal descent of the bindus. Getting up, stirring up, working up, keying up, and whipping up are all synonyms of how we get up and about in our diurnal ascent as the bindus arise. Likewise, in this human race to nowhere, we're always trying to speed up, hurry up, move up, and catch up, which often results in our heating up, cranking up, and eventually blowing up. The healing prescription for all of this is to try to calm down, cool down, settle down, quiet down, or otherwise slow down, which essentially means settling the winds and dropping from your head into your body.

When we can't calm down, the result is insomnia.

According to Tibetan inner yoga, when you dream, the drops come up from the heart chakra and reside in the throat chakra. In the Kabbalah, the mystical aspect of Judaism, the throat center is also associated with dreaming. Dreaming consciousness is a sort of halfway house between the full waking state (at the head) and the deep dreamless state (at the heart). When dreaming, you come halfway up, but not all the way up to waking consciousness. This halfway point at the throat is the inner target for lucid dreaming and dream yoga.

The inner yoga approaches work to consciously move the winds and drops into these chakras in an effort to *lucidly* bring about these three states of consciousness. The movement of these winds and drops happens spontaneously when we sleep, dream, and then awaken, but in the untrained mind it happens without awareness, or non-lucidly. We lose consciousness as we slip and fall into sleep. Meditation masters do not lose consciousness; they are able to sustain awareness or lucidity through all states.

These subtle forms of yoga show us that the only thing we lose as we slip and fall into sleep is gross outer waking consciousness. The inner practices allow us to *find* subtle states of consciousness that we descend into every night when we drop into sleep and dream. A natural consequence of this finding is lucidity in the dream state.

The practice of the inner yogas of sleep and dream is based on this principle: where the mind goes, the winds go; where the winds of the inner yogas go, the drops go; where the drops go, so goes consciousness. What directs the winds to these chakras and constitutes a major aspect of inner yoga (also called "wind yoga") is visualization and chanting. Through visualizing these different colored chakras and chanting their respective "sounds," a yogi moves or stretches consciousness to these locations and thereby to the states of consciousness they represent.

By visualizing, feeling, or imagining these chakras, you are guiding the winds and drops to these spots, a technique called "penetrating the vital points." The vital points are the chakras, and the yogi penetrates the states of consciousness contained therein. It's an Eastern form of hacking. In this case, you're breaking and entering into the previously impenetrable (unconscious or non-lucid) states of dream and sleep.

With this understanding of the subtle body, we can now introduce some Eastern induction techniques that rely on it, starting with a more subtle understanding of good sleep hygiene. Without this long-winded introduction, the following practices would be meaningless. Remember, the preliminaries are more important than the main practice.

EXERCISE: The Sleeping Lion

This passive technique is called the "sleeping lion posture," the posture the Buddha allegedly assumed when he died. It's commonly depicted in paintings and sculptures throughout Asia. In yogic language, this *mudra* or *asana* is conducive to lucid dreams. When you go to sleep tonight, lie down on your right side with your legs slightly bent, rest your left arm on top of your left side, and (if it works for you) block off your right nostril by crooking your right arm and pressing your fist of nonaggression against your nose.

The wind that flows through the right channel is called *sun poison prana*, and it's considered a "masculine" and extroverted wind. This prana is "bad breath" in the world of dream yoga, because when the winds flow through this channel they tend to keep you awake. The next time you wake up in the middle of the night or find yourself wrestling with insomnia, check which nostril you're breathing through. You will often find that you're breathing through your right nostril. Try rolling over onto your right side and pressing that nostril closed. See if this works for you, then journal what you discover.

_____

_____

_____

_____

The wind that flows through the left channel is called *moon nectar prana*, and it's considered a "feminine" and introverted wind. According to inner yoga, we want to sleep, dream, and even die in a more "feminine" state of mind. By taking the sleeping lion posture, we're inviting the closure of the outward-bound right channel, and inviting the opening of the inward-bound left channel.

The sleeping lion posture is a method unto itself, but it can also be assumed as a baseline posture for any other induction method. Another traditional technique is to sleep sitting up, like when you doze off on a plane. This tends to lead to a lighter sleep, which is conducive to lucidity. See if these techniques work for you (and don't worry if they don't; they're not for everybody). Then journal what you notice.

_____

_____

_____

_____

Unwinding

When we come home from work, settle into the evening, and then eventually prepare for sleep, we're slowly unwinding. From a subtle body point of view, we're actually un-*wind*ing. We're letting the winds settle down. The Western necktie has become a symbol for how we choke off the winds (and therefore the drops) into the head chakra, wind ourselves up, and then suffer all the associated head disorders, like watery eyes, headaches, insomnia, tinnitus (ringing of the ears), and a host of other ailments. The necktie has turned into a noose, and it is "hanging up" many men. When I look at the baggy eyes of sleep-deprived businessmen, it's as if those bags are inflated by the subtle winds that are strangled there.

With our evening meditation, we're untying the inner necktie and allowing the winds and drops to descend. If the winds didn't settle, they would keep us *up* all night.

EXERCISE: The Black Pearls

If you suffer from insomnia or any other condition that keeps you up, try this inner yoga trick. Visualize two black pearls, one at the bottom of each foot. Try to really feel them there, firm and cool. Bring the pearls to life by noticing how they glisten and almost tingle. Visualization is equally *feelingization*. It's not just cognitive, but also visceral. Take a moment to feel into this visualization now. It helps to keep your attention actively moving around the pearls, thus injecting energy into them. If you keep your attention too solidly fixed, the mind tends to stray. Try keeping your mind fixed on the black pearls. Write down what you experience.

_____

_____

_____

_____

By bringing your attention to the bottom of your feet, you're bringing the winds there, drawing your consciousness down. This is part of a family of meditations called "the extreme path to the middle." The middle in this instance is the heart chakra, where the mind resides in deep sleep. The first extreme is the mind being too up, stuck in the head chakra. The second extreme, which works to balance the first, is placing your attention down at your feet. The goal is to bring the winds and drops into the heart chakra, and this practice (called "subterranean samadhi") can help you do so. Try it and see if it works for you. But don't get too hung up about it if it doesn't.

After settling your mind for a few minutes with regular meditation, you can clean up your act before bed even further with the following ninefold purification breathing practice. It's a terrific way to blow out the cylinders, so to speak, and to set the stage for lucid sleep onset.

EXERCISE: Ninefold Purification Breathing

This practice is also called "expelling the stale air," and it is particularly helpful when you find yourself all wound up. It's also useful for severe bouts of insomnia, when nothing seems to be able to settle you down. The idea is to completely clear out all the stale prana. Sit in meditation posture, with an upright spine and your hands in the fist of nonaggression described earlier. The thumb pressing on the base of the ring finger closes a subtle channel that is associated with discursive or speedy thoughts. You're putting the brakes on the winds that flow through that nadi.

Of the several variations, this is one of the most common. (Tips: Before you begin, blow your nose so it is clear. Doing each breath cycle slowly and deliberately prevents you from hyperventilating.)

1. Block your right nostril with your right index finger.

2. Take a deep in-breath through your left nostril and when your lungs are fully inflated, pause.

3. Start the out-breath slowly, then at the end of the exhalation forcefully expel every last wisp of air, and splay out the fingers of your left hand.

4. Feel the stale wind being expelled not only through your left nostril but also through every pore of your body. There's a sense of blowing out all the stale air in your lungs and in your subtle body.

5. Do this once, then write down how it feels.

_____

_____

6. Do this cycle three times, then write down how it feels.

_____

_____

7. For the next three breaths, block off the left nostril with your left index finger, and repeat as above.

8. For three final breaths, keep both hands on your thighs and repeat as above, but now exhale through both nostrils, splaying out the fingers of both hands.

How does it feel after you do these last two sets of exhalations?

_____

_____

Check into the quality and speediness of your mind before and after this exercise. Does your mind clear out as the winds clear out? Is your mind less "windy" at the end? Journal what you experience.

_____

_____

_____

_____

As you continue this practice over time, track how things change in your journal.

The Power of Visualization

The exercises in this chapter fully engage the power of visualization, or imagination, to induce lucidity, employing the tenets of the subtle body as we have discussed. It's helpful to "prepare the bed" for these practices with the following sequence.

EXERCISE: Throat Visualization

1. When you go to bed, lie down on your back and put your hands on your belly. This will help you ground your mind and bring the winds down.

2. Counteract any tendency to get too loose or sloppy as you lie down by being a bit tight at first. Count twenty-one breaths, each cycle of in-breath and out-breath counting as one breath. What do you notice after you do this?

_____

_____

_____

3. After the twenty-one breaths, bring your awareness to your throat by visualizing a red pearl there. You can replace the pearl with a red AH (a seed syllable in yogic language). Remember that red is the color of this chakra, and AH is its sound. Gently but resolutely hold your mind there for a few minutes, then let everything go and allow yourself to drift into sleep. You can do this either remaining in the same supine posture or assuming the sleeping lion posture. See what feels right for you. Journal what you experience:

_____

_____

Visualization practice is connected to shamanic journeying and also to the practice of *active imagination*, as described by Carl Jung (who used it as a bridge from the conscious to the unconscious mind). In tantric Buddhism, visualization constitutes an entire family of practices referred to as *generation stage meditation*. With lucid dreaming, visualization is another "twofer" practice—you're getting two benefits for the price of one. The first benefit is using visualization as an inner yoga, transitioning awareness from gross waking consciousness to subtle dreaming consciousness, as in the preceding and following exercises.

The second benefit: visualization stabilizes the mind. We can practice visualization during the day and see the fruits of our practice at night. As your mind stabilizes with daytime visualization practices, and that stabilized mind is then released into the dream state, your dreams will become more stable. Visualization also works to clarify and sharpen the mind, which bears fruit in your dreams. So daytime visualization works to clarify, sharpen, and stabilize the mind, which results in clearer, sharper, and more stable dreams. You're exercising a similar mental muscle—day or night.

EXERCISE: Visualize This

This is a mindfulness meditation that serves to stabilize your awareness. Grab a red marker or pen and draw a four-petaled red lotus, as large or as small as you wish. Concentrate on the line as you outline the lotus, being mindful as you make each "lap." Try not to be distracted as you draw the lotus.

Can you draw it once without being distracted? How about going over the same lines a second time? What happens when you sketch it quickly? How about slowly? Write down what you experience.

_____

_____

Once you get a feel for this, close your eyes and draw the red lotus with the "pen" of your mind's eye by visualizing the lotus in the space in front of you. Visualize the red lotus as clearly as you can, and mentally draw it over and over. It helps to inject some energy into the visualization by making the lotus three-dimensional. Bring it to life and make it flutter. You don't want this to be a mere cognitive exercise. You want to infuse the visualization with some feeling and vibrancy. Journal how this feels to you.

_____

_____

_____

Is it difficult or easy? Is it hard to draw the lotus without being distracted? Does it help to go faster or slower?

_____

_____

What happens when you inject the visualization with enthusiasm and energy?

_____

_____

After you get a feel for this practice, move the visualization of the red lotus down to your throat. Draw it over and over, and make it as red and real as you can. Feel the lotus quiver. This stage also serves to stimulate the throat chakra and acts as a bridge into the next and final exercise. Is it easier or harder to visualize the lotus in your throat? Try gently holding your Adam's apple with either hand. Does that help you sustain awareness in your throat? Now move your fingers and massage your throat. How does that affect your visualization?

_____

_____

Infusing the visualization with feeling brings it to life, which then helps you bring it into your dreams. It's not hard to imagine or visualize a new lover, or the vacation you're dreaming about, or that new car you want. Our feelings naturally energize those images. That's the level of energy you want to bring to this practice, which is another way to add octane to your intent. In Eastern terms, it's a way to step up the karma, which is always driven by intent.

For many Westerners, visualization practice may seem contrived at first, but it's been used by the wisdom traditions for thousands of years. Motivational speakers constantly proclaim the benefits of powerful visualization and echo the words of the Bengali poet Rabindranath Tagore: "The stronger the imagination, the less imaginary the results."

Once again, you'll see it when you *believe* it. You'll see the results of this practice once you really buy into it. And one of the best ways to develop this belief is to just do it. Stick with it. Watch your daytime visualization become clear, sharp, and stable, and you'll witness your dreams doing the same. This is why journaling your experience is important, even if you initially experience nothing. You'll be able to track your progress.

In the tantric texts, it is said that visualization masters with sharp and steady minds can visualize a hundred deities in the space of a sesame seed. These are mental Olympians who then reap the rewards of all their training by having constant lucid dreams. These proclamations are meant not to intimidate you but to inspire you for what is possible. The mind has astounding capabilities—if it is exercised.

EXERCISE: Drawing the Lotus

As another refinement, and the way to take all this to bed, start as in the "Throat Visualization" exercise:

1. When you lie down to sleep, put your hands on your belly and count twenty-one breaths.

2. Now visualize the four-petaled red lotus in your throat.

3. Draw the outline of the lotus with your mind's eye, going around several times.

4. Then settle your mind on the front petal, the petal that is facing out from your throat. As you start to doze off, bring your mind to the petal on the right and gently hold it there, drawing that petal back and forth in your mind's eye.

5. When you get even sleepier, switch to the petal in the back and briefly hold your mind there.

At this point you're dipping in and out of sleep, and it's getting harder to hold onto the petal with your mind's eye. The "pen" of your mind is frequently lifting off the "page." You're in the hypnagogic state, heading toward Hypnos, the god of sleep.

6. When you're really losing it, move to the petal on the left and briefly alight your fading awareness there. Now you're really losing your grip on waking consciousness and slipping into sleep.

7. When you can barely hold on, the final step is to bring your awareness to the center of the lotus and let go. Drop everything and fall into sleep.

Journal what you discover, either in the morning or, if you wake up, right after you do this. How did this go for you? How far did you get in drawing the lotus? Did your mind wander, or did you feel too sleepy to focus?

_____

_____

_____

_____

This exercise is revelatory. If it doesn't speak to you or you just can't do it, don't judge yourself. The lotus visualization comes from the dream yoga tradition and is the most subtle and advanced practice in this book. If it does resonate with you and you stay with it, this "descent visualization" can really help you advance into nighttime lucidity. Even if you can't do it, just trying is a way of bringing awareness into the night, a potent practice of lucid sleep onset.

This nuanced meditation guides you through four increasingly subtle steps into sleep. It brings a refined structure to a process that is usually free-form and inarticulate, installing the "dimmer" we discussed earlier. With practice, you will learn how to keep a few "photons" of lucidity on as you slide into sleep. Remember, we're introducing practices that are designed to match the subtlety of the mind as it descends into sleep.

This practice takes time and patience, and your experience can vary from night to night, depending on how tired you are. If you're exhausted, you'll step down the lotus quickly. When you're not so tired, it can take a few minutes to step yourself into sleep. Try it for a few weeks and see how it goes for you, then write down your experience.

_____

_____

QUESTIONS AND ANSWERS

Does regular outer body yoga, like ashtanga or hatha yoga, work with the subtle body?

Yes. But these yoga methods (and many other outer body practices) do not target the subtle body as directly as inner yoga does. In accordance with the tenets of bidirectionality, we're always working with the subtle body, whether we know it or not. This means that even your regular meditation is working with your subtle body. When the mind works on the body, that is *downward causation*; when the body works on the mind, that is *upward causation*. By becoming more aware of this mutually causative process, we can effect transformation in either direction more rapidly.

Are there any risks to working with the subtle body?

The subtle body has great potential to effect positive or negative transformation at outer levels. But the good news is that the entry-level inner yoga methods discussed here are very safe. The risks come with inappropriate use of more advanced inner yoga techniques.

Is the subtle body it? Or is there something even more subtle?

Within or below the subtle body is a very subtle body that is actually formless, and according to the wisdom traditions, it gives rise to both the subtle and the gross body. This very subtle body is what we inhabit when we fall into deep dreamless (formless) sleep, the deepest meditations, and death. In the West it is often referred to as "soul." Sleep yoga works with this very subtle body (which abides in the heart center), as do formless meditations designed to prepare you for death (bardo yoga). While the gross body is "loud," and the subtle body is "quiet," the very subtle body is totally silent. These three bodies are the simplest formulations of what lies within us. Other traditions posit other bodies, such as the *five koshas* of Hinduism.

Part III

What to Do with Lucid Dreams

CHAPTER 10

General Obstacles and Solutions

Lucid dreaming has boundless potential, but along with that promise there are obstacles, both general and specific, internal and external. If we understand the hurdles, we'll be able to negotiate them. With the proper lens, obstacles are really opportunities in disguise, and rather than obstructing growth can actually facilitate it. As one dream yoga master put it, "Obstacles don't obstruct the path—they *are* the path." We'll start with the outer and more general obstacles, and then focus on the inner and more specific challenges.

Understanding and transforming the general obstacles is more important than working with the particulars (like how to extend a lucid dream, what to do to end a dream, and so on). This sustains the overarching spirit of lucid dreaming, whereby the preliminaries are more important than the main practice. If you work with the general obstacles, many of the specific hindrances take care of themselves.

Like dreams themselves, many of the obstacles occur at unconscious levels. That's what makes them formidable. They work underground, and their subversive power is directly proportional to how deep and unconscious they are. When we're working with the unconscious mind, we're working with blind spots. These blind spots include biases and prejudices so hidden in the shadows that sometimes we don't even see that we don't see. Therefore, the first general solution is to understand and appreciate the "forces of the dark side" and to smile at all of it.

What allows us to convert obstacle into opportunity is largely the right attitude. So nurture a sense of adventure, the courage to walk into the dark, the willingness to be exposed, the perseverance to continue in the face of adversity, and the humor that embraces this nocturnal project. If you fill your backpack with these qualities, you will succeed on the journey into lucidity.

Once again, dreaming in general, and lucid dreaming in particular, is revelatory. Learning about all these obstacles is similarly revealing and can teach you a great deal about yourself. As you explore the difficulties that accompany the lucid dreaming venture, you may discover all sorts of blinders, and then remove them. A successful oneironaut (a person who explores dream worlds) is one who celebrates this exposure. This is the spirit we should adopt as we head into the dark and bring these obstacles into light.

Take a moment to jot down how this settles with you. Are you up for these revelations? How much do you really want to learn about yourself?

_____

_____

SOCIAL AND CULTURAL OBSTACLES

One of the biggest obstacles is Western society's generally dismissive relationship to dreams. "It's only a dream" is a frequent and trivializing comment in Western culture. In the Western world, dreams are considered not as real as waking reality, and therefore not as important. What's important is waking consciousness, and what we can control.

Has your attitude about dreams changed since you started reading this book? If so, what brought about that change? If not, what needs to happen to make this change?

_____

_____

We need to realize that this is merely a Western view of reality, a shortsighted view that is actually in the minority. Aside from Western European and European-derived societies, there are over four thousand cultures in the world, and about 90 percent of them value experiences gleaned from altered states of consciousness, especially those gathered from dreams. In many cultures, dreams are regarded as different aspects of reality—not unreality. In these cultures, anthropologist Charles D. Laughlin writes, "Dream experiences, just as waking experiences, inform the society's general system of knowledge about the self and the world, as well as the development of a person's identity."[35]

In the Eastern view, if you're lucid to dreams, they are actually *more* in contact with reality than waking consciousness. This is why meditating in a dream is up to nine times more effective than meditating when awake. And as unbelievable as it may seem, being lucid in deep dreamless sleep—which many of us may never experience and therefore find hard to imagine—is when we're in most direct contact with reality. Of this, the Indian sage Ramana Maharshi observed, "That which does not exist in deep dreamless sleep is not real."

So raise your gaze, and look beyond the nearsighted view from the West. Read books about dreams from *polyphasic cultures* (which value altered states of consciousness, including experiences from the dream world). Look into accounts of societies that honor dreams and spiritual traditions that treasure them. Anthropologist Tara Lumpkin argues that *monophasic* cultures like ours limit "perceptual diversity," which is one of the subtle forms of prejudice alluded to earlier. Acknowledge this lack of diversity—a sneaky form of discrimination that favors waking consciousness—and work to remedy it.

If you think you are a member of a monophasic culture, consider how diversified your view of reality is, and the extent of your bias toward waking consciousness. Explore this here:

_____

_____

_____

_____

_____

Wake-Centricity

One of the most sinister obstacles to lucid dreaming, which is also a cultural by-product, is our partiality to waking consciousness. This is largely a problem in human development, because it is related to the ego, which is actually a form of arrested development. The ego holds many biases, and wake-centricity is foremost among them. Ego is fully operational and online only in the waking state; it dissolves as we fall asleep. The ego therefore dismisses other states of consciousness it can't fully experience, like the dreaming state.

Waking consciousness dominates our experience as much as the ego dominates our lives. If the ego can't experience something in broad daylight, it reasons that something must not be real. "Ego" refers to a specific developmental level that is self-centric, body based, and just one rung on the developmental ladder from dirt to divinity. Those with big egos in the colloquial sense are those who inflate the characteristics of this developmental level. The egoic level of human evolution is seduced and blinded by external light, which draws us out and away from our darker, deeper self, where dreams abide. This is another reason the gross ego tends to dismiss subtle states it can't recognize.

Do you think that what you experience during the day is more valid than what you experience at night? If so, write down why you find your daytime experiences more authentic.

_____

_____

_____

_____

Wake-centricity is behind the assumption that the only way to know reality is through our outward physical senses and the thinking mind that appropriates and coordinates their data. But it's a closed-minded way to look at reality, a limited view that leaves out two essential states of reality. As Lumpkin writes, "[T]he entire system of consciousness is far more complex and, in breaking it down and valuing only one of its parts, waking rational consciousness, one loses the value of the whole."[36] The other two essential states, which complete the whole, are the subtle consciousness of the dreaming state and the very subtle awareness of the deep dreamless sleep state. For meditation masters who live with full lucidity in all states of consciousness, the experience of dreaming and sleeping states is just as viable as the experience of the waking state.

Because waking consciousness is the only state in which ego can fully experience reality, it has invested its entire portfolio in this one bandwidth of experience. To challenge the error of this investment strategy is to challenge the ego itself. So lucid dreaming (especially the more advanced transpersonal and therefore trans-egoic stages, where the goal is to no longer protect or inflate the ego) presents an affront to the ego by contesting its limited worldview, confronting its perceptual bias, and disputing its claim on awareness. And the ego, which is defined by drawing boundaries, relates to this affront as a security breach, a threat to its dominance or even to its very existence. At a deep unconscious level, *the ego knows that the nocturnal meditations, by dissolving boundaries, might dissolve the ego.*

How does this settle with you? Does this assertion make you feel somewhat uneasy, or does it feel liberating, even refreshing?

_____

_____

Recall that lucid dreaming is sometimes referred to as "dream hacking." At deeper levels of practice, lucid dreaming is also a way to hack into the ego and disrupt its operating system. Are you up for being so disrupted? If not, why not?

While the initial levels of lucid dreaming aren't that threatening to the ego, its evolution into dream yoga is a different story. Dream yoga is designed to upset ego's antiquated operating system, and update our files to include the other two states of dreaming and sleeping consciousness.

The structure of the ego is loosened at higher stages of lucid dreaming, and it completely dissolves in dream yoga and sleep yoga. Paraphrasing the meditation master Trungpa Rinpoche: you can't attend your own funeral.

Ego can't attend egoless/dreamless states, so on a deep level it fears these states. Nocturnal meditations are therefore a threat to the ego, even though that threat may not be fully recognized or articulated. For the ego, something just feels off with these deeper practices. But when we discover that "death" at a lower level of development allows for birth and transcendence into a higher level, we find the courage to let go, or "die."

Settle into this claim, and write down whether this promise of transcendence replaces any anxiety with a feeling of anticipation. Do you feel the excitement of new possibilities, of growth beyond the ego?

The first way past the obstacle of wake-centricity is to realize, again, that ego is a form of arrested development, and that growth continues into trans-egoic realms. By discovering ego's place in the spectrum of human development, you'll be more likely to release your grip on it. Developmental studies, evolutionary psychology, transpersonal disciplines, and integral psychology are ways to stabilize this inner view of growth, and help you understand the developmental role of the nocturnal meditations.

The second way past this obstacle is to realize that waking consciousness is indeed just part of the picture. There is so much more of life you'll be living when you embrace the lucid experiences of the dreaming and dreamless sleep states.

No Role Models

Another barrier to lucid dreaming is the lack of role models. Can you think of a lucid dreaming authority figure or a person you admire in the world of lucid dreaming?

_____

_____

There are academic, scientific, and spiritual pioneers in this field, but most of them fly below our cultural radar. Most lucid dreamers are slashing their way through the undergrowth, relying on their own experience, putting their faith in a few books, and banking on the occasional seminar. Young scientists are discouraged from pursuing a career in lucid dreaming; it is the rare scholar that ventures to study these special dreams, and dream yoga masters shun the limelight. When the scientist Ursula Voss was first approached by an elder dream researcher and asked about collaborating, she admits thinking, *Oh no! Let's do something more scientific.* Voss later relented and has since become one of the most influential lucid dreaming scientists.[37]

How many of your friends have heard about lucid dreaming, let alone dream yoga? Outside of the movie *Inception*, can you think of a film that features lucid dreaming?

_____

_____

Don't discount the power of peer pressure. Our peers can either lift us up or take us down. Are you a bit shy, or even embarrassed, to bring the topic of lucid dreaming up to others? If it excites you—and if you've read this far, I'm betting that it does—what is it about lucid dreaming that gets you going?

_____

_____

Nocturnal meditations are solitary by nature. You can't take anybody with you as you journey into the darkness of the night. There are no role models. The cultural and social support isn't there. Peer pressure is real. Lucid dreaming is a pioneering endeavor, and you have to be willing to face these pressures and remain steadfast.

One antidote to negative peer pressure is finding support communities (try Reddit, or my own Night Club community). As the benefits of lucid dreaming continue to grow, so too does the subculture of lucid dreamers.

INTERNAL OBSTACLES

From the day we are born, the external obstacles gradually become internalized, until they lurk in the shadows of the unconscious mind, exerting a silent but prodigious influence on our conscious lives. It's relatively easy to point out, acknowledge, and therefore blame outside influences, but when we look inside, the forces of the dark side become nearly pitch black. Internal obstacles are therefore more challenging to deal with, but also proportionally more rewarding when we do so successfully.

These internal forces are like powerful lobbyists wandering the halls of our unconscious mind, wielding their influence to create the cognitive and perceptual laws that restrict much of our conscious experience. Operating on the principle of bidirectionality, this conscious experience then downloads into the unconscious mind, restricting what we experience there. In other words, these same internal laws dictate how we dream. By bringing these internal dictates into the light of conscious awareness, we can establish a new relationship to them and start to illuminate our dreams.

First, we must acknowledge the full spectrum of our identity. Gaining a deeper understanding of identity structure, of who you are and how you express yourself, will help you relate to these different aspects of yourself.

Have you ever taken a close look and asked the question, *Who am I?* Set this book down and reflect on this ageless inquiry. Do you think that you operate on just one frequency of identity? Or are you a composite of many momentary selves?

_____

_____

_____

We don't function on just one bandwidth of identity. We're spread across a spectrum of being, from "infrared" to "ultraviolet," from beast to Buddha. The infrared aspects of ourselves are gross, selfish, debased, ignorant, and prefer to sleep; the ultraviolet aspects are subtle, selfless, refined, wise, and long to wake up. This higher bandwidth is at the forefront of your evolution, tugging at the rest of you to come along.

Pause for a moment and pat yourself on the back. But be careful to not let your aspirations for growth paradoxically inflate your ego. Do you feel dangerously close to self-aggrandizement? Is there a tinge of superiority lurking in the shadows of your psychological and spiritual aspirations for evolution?

_____

_____

The leading edge of your identity is the gas pedal of your development, propelling you forward into the future. But the caboose in your identity train can hold you back with tons of historical baggage. This caboose is heavy, because it carries all your habitual patterns. In James Joyce's *Ulysses*, Stephen Dedalus declares, "History is a nightmare from which I am trying to awake." The infrared part of you whispers defeatist comments like, *Lucid dreaming is not for you. It's a waste of time*, or *You can't do this; it's too subtle and advanced*, or *I'm too busy for this; let's get on with something that's real.* The doubt is compounded when external forces continue to support that story line. Do you find yourself whispering defeatist comments like these? If so, write them here and explore why you feel this way.

_____

_____

_____

_____

The solution is to first discover this spectrum of identity, which is a spectrum of consciousness itself, and to acknowledge the power of your evolutionary tail. But don't let it wag the dog. When the doubts come, let them go. When the internal critic speaks, don't listen. If you just keep going and let the force of evolution take over, sooner or later all the baggage falls away, and you will travel more lightly and freely into the future.

Human development, and the path to lucidity, is largely about what to accept (the ultraviolet) and what to reject (the infrared). The practice is twofold: first, to identify your less-evolved bandwidth of identity, then work to let it go; and second, to identify your more-evolved bandwidth, then nurture it.

The next exercise does just that, revealing the part of you that doesn't want to become lucid and the part that is bringing you to lucidity. This is revelatory—and often humbling.

EXERCISE: Infrared and Ultraviolet

Take a few minutes—or hours or days—to recall some instances in the recent past when you were selfish or did something with disregard for others. Describe these infrared thoughts and actions:

_____

_____

_____

_____

_____

Don't chastise yourself; realize that these attitudes and actions are just your caboose.

Now take a few minutes, hours, or days to recall instances in the recent past when you were selfless in thought or deed and did things with consideration for others. Describe these ultraviolet thoughts and actions:

_____

_____

_____

_____

_____

Acknowledge and celebrate this part of you; nurture it. Realize that these thoughts and acts represent your evolutionary engine.

Lucid dreaming can help you become aware of who you really are, at what "frequencies" you spend most of your life, and thereby facilitate the transition from non-lucid frequencies to lucid frequencies. Some people savor this revelation; others dread it. Where do you fit in? How do you feel about this exercise?

_____

_____

Force of Habit

Of all the forces that keep us non-lucid, perhaps the most seemingly intractable is the force of habit. Habits generate our defaults, our automatic reactions to life. Habits also create the givens or axioms of our life, the things we take for granted or don't even think about questioning.

To give you a playful sense of the power of habit, try brushing your teeth with your nondominant hand, or copying this sentence, word by word, from the opposite direction, going from right to left here:

_____

_____

Probably not so easy. The forces of non-lucidity are even more formidable.

For most people, it's a given that all dreams are non-lucid, which is why it can be so stunning when we finally have a lucid dream. Most of us also don't realize that this axiomatic view of non-lucidity is indeed a given, in the sense that it was unintentionally *given* to us by our parents, friends, peers, and virtually everyone else in the non-lucid world.

This implies that habit (or karma) is not just individual but also collective. The individual and the collective generate and reinforce habits for each other. The self is a product of society, and society is a collective product of selves. So habit delivers a double whammy: it's both internal and external, both individual and collective.

Remember that we're always meditating, always becoming increasingly familiar with mindlessness or mindfulness, non-lucidity or lucidity. And so we're either adding fuel to our evolutionary engine or loading our devolutionary caboose. Habit is a good news/bad news scenario. We can either let the power of habit continue to force us into non-lucidity or harness it to force ourselves into lucidity. A large part of this book is about taking the latter action.

One of the most unsettling discoveries for aspiring lucid dreamers is realizing their hidden desire for non-lucidity. This devolutionary habit continues to accrete every time we succumb to the force of distraction, or cave in to mindlessness, or space out in forgetfulness—all synonyms for non-lucidity. We even pay for it. We love to get lost at the movies, and the entertainment industry is a multi-billion-dollar success story in distraction, or non-lucidity. The really dark aspect of this industry is that the movies are not just external, but also internal.

Every time a thought moves within our mind and we get drawn into it, we're buying into the mindlessness industry. Every time an emotion carries us away, we're investing in non-lucidity. We may not pay for this level of distraction in hard currency, but we end up paying for it with the currency of attention, which means it eventually costs us our lives. The quality of our life is the cost for being so seduced into the infinite forms of non-lucidity.

EXERCISE: The Lure of Distraction

Take a candid look at your life and ask yourself how much you enjoy being distracted. How often do you allow yourself to drift away into a reverie, float off into a daydream, or get swept along with a fantasy?

_____

_____

_____

The practice of mindfulness (lucidity) meditation interrupts this agenda, so here's the second part of this exercise: how annoying is it to keep coming back to the present moment? How does this practice of lucidity—of striving to be completely present all the time—feel to you?

_____

_____

_____

_____

I'm not implying that reverie, daydreaming, and fantasies are inherently bad. I'm just trying to bring our unconscious default habits into the light of conscious awareness. This is another "twofer" exercise, because it simultaneously reveals yet again why we're so good at non-lucidity, and what we need to do to become lucid. It's hard to change habits. But it's virtually impossible if we don't even know what we have to change.

The principle solution to the force of habit is first understanding the magnitude of this force and then developing the patience required to change it. Whether you know it or not, you've been practicing, and even paying for, non-lucidity most of your life. So give yourself a break. Marvel at the force of habit and how proficient you are in non-lucidity. It took time to develop all this non-lucid momentum, and it will take some time to exhaust it. The most advanced lucid dreamers never give up. That's how they advance. And trust me: you can, too.

CHAPTER 11

Specific Obstacles and Solutions

With our discussion of general obstacles behind us, we can now examine more specific obstacles, which are easier to deal with because they're usually more conscious. When someone steps onto the path of lucidity, they tend to go through three phases. These phases don't always unfold in a sequential order, and not everybody will experience them. You can bounce among all three phases, only experience one or two, or experience all three in short order. But sooner or later most people experience some version of the following.

First is the *manic* phase. You've done the research, read the books, and maybe had your first lucid dream. You've caught the fever and just can't get enough. This phase can last for months, years, or even an entire lifetime. Have you experienced this phase? If so, what sold you? If not, what do you think needs to happen?

_____

_____

_____

As with most endeavors, the mania often disappears, and you enter the second phase. This is the *conflicted* phase, when doubts creep in and the weight of the devolutionary caboose drags you down. Maybe your friends were right when they said you're wasting your time. Maybe that inner voice that says you can't do this is accurate. You still have moments when the highs return, but they now alternate with the lows. If you think you've experienced this, describe how it's felt for you:

_____

_____

When you're in the conflicted phase, it helps to understand the spectrum of your identity. There's a conflict of interest here. Conscious and unconscious forces are not in harmony, and that conflict is rearing its head. If you cave in to the lows and capitulate to old habits, you'll eventually drop out.

The third phase is the *mature* phase. Because you've hung in there long enough to have some success, you understand what's required to become lucid. You realize that lucid dreaming is not a sprint, but more like a marathon. This maturity allows you to relax. You're now evenly balanced between "too tight" and "too loose." You also realize that lucid dreaming is not linear. Like an incoming tide that advances and recedes as it gradually moves forward, lucidity has similar surges that are part of the path. You might have droughts when you hardly even remember a dream, let alone have a lucid dream. But you remember that lucidity is like heating that vat of cold water, so you keep putting energy into the system even though nothing seems to be happening. You understand that beneath the exterior, things are heating up, so you remain steadfast in your efforts.

Do you relate to this description? If you feel like you've entered the "desert" of lucid dreaming, or ups and downs like a gyrating stock market, use this space to vent—and to offer yourself support and encouragement for the long haul:

_____

_____

_____

_____

DISCOURAGEMENT

Discouragement is one of the biggest obstacles. The causes are legion: lucid dreaming is too hard or too subtle, too advanced or too disruptive. *I don't have the time; I'm not cut out for this; I just can't do it. It's just not worth the trouble.* The good news is that there are as many solutions to despair as there are reasons to quit. Where are you with discouragement? Are you feeling disheartened? Does lucid dreaming feel hopeless? If so, why?

_____

_____

_____

The first solution is to understand all the reasons why lucid dreaming takes time, which is why we've spent so much time on this topic. Then cultivate the patience, determination, and humor that fuels progress.

Second, celebrate your small successes. Remembering more of your dreams? Fantastic! Are you having clearer and more frequent dreams? Rejoice! Did you have a lucid dreamlet or a glimpse of lucid dreaming? That's amazing! As always, a dream journal helps you track your progress, like a parent marking lines on a doorframe to measure their child's growth. Are you having some of these successes? Review your journal entries in this book, and briefly note your development.

While expectation is important, don't set the bar too high. You'll never measure up if you expect instant results.

Third, let your failures teach you. In the world of lucid dreaming, obstacles are opportunities in disguise. Not being able to accomplish the various aspects of lucid dreaming will successfully reveal your blind spots and the places where you're stuck. I continue to flounder at many of the stages of lucid dreaming, and these unsuccessful attempts show me precisely where I need to apply my efforts, or where my unconscious habits still dominate. These failures are teachable moments that point the way to success.

Where are you having the biggest problems with lucid dreaming? Write them down individually—and realize that everybody faces challenges.

By teasing apart the various strands of difficulty, you take a "divide and conquer" approach. It's easy to get discouraged by a heap of problems if they're all lumped together. Non-lucidity comes about in a systemic way, with a host of factors conspiring to keep us in the dark. Lucidity also comes about in a systemic way. By identifying the individual factors you can address them individually, which eventually adds up to a heap of encouraging success.

Fourth, while you want to take lucid dreaming seriously, don't take it *too* seriously. You can tie yourself into knots by trying too hard. It helps to view lucid dreaming playfully, almost as a game. So relax and lighten up. Have fun. And don't be afraid to take a break. If you find yourself in the "too tight" camp, stressing out about not having lucid dreams, what are some ways you could loosen up and relieve the pressure?

_____

_____

_____

_____

While lucid dreaming and dream yoga may be the "measure of the path" for *yourself*, it's important not to use your successes and failures to measure yourself against others. We're all different. Each of us has a unique set of faculties and foibles. Don't compare yourself to others. Trust your own uniqueness; take refuge in your innate wisdom. Let others lift you up, but don't allow them to take you down.

BEING TOO EXCITED

People often get so excited when they have their first lucid dreams that they wake themselves up. The solution is to temper your emotions. In the world of lucid dreaming, rationality supersedes emotionality. When you find yourself lucid in your dream, look down at the ground or floor of your dream, and *then* engage the dream. Sensory engagement with the dream discourages the brain from changing states to waking consciousness. A useful tip is to rub your dream hands together. Take a moment to do this right now, to literally get a feel for this tip.

Just as engaging your waking world in the morning pulls you out of your dream and into the world, engaging in your dreams pulls you into your dream and out of waking reality. The beginning of lucidity is also a good time to remember your goals for the dream, what you want to accomplish tonight. Write down what you want to do in your lucid dream tonight (flying, romantic encounter—anything), and infuse this with strong intention.

_____

_____

_____

The next exercise works with the maxim that "rationality supersedes emotionality" and serves to extend the lucidity principle into life.

EXERCISE: From Emotion to Daytime Lucidity

The next time you find yourself in an emotional situation during the day, "wake up" and try to temper your emotions. Notice the force of habit that sucks you into the emotion, and how easy it is to lose it in non-lucidity. Then take a deep breath or another purposeful action to keep yourself from getting too involved with what's happening. Step back. Then journal how successful you were in the space provided. Did the emotion get the better of you, or were you able to "hold your seat" and remain unmoved?

_____

_____

_____

_____

This doesn't mean you get rid of your emotions or dissociate from your feelings; rather, it means that you control your relationship to them. Dream control is essentially self-control, and that's something you can practice during the day.

This daily practice of lucidity is one of the most practical benefits of lucid dreaming. "Waking up" to your emotional states not only helps you wake up to your dreams, but it can also keep you out of a heap of trouble by helping you establish a more lucid relationship to your mind in charged situations. Are you about to say something you're going to regret? Or do something you'll have to apologize for? Wake up and take control of your thoughts and feelings. Record the next instance this daily practice of lucidity gets you out of trouble.

_____

_____

_____

_____

As you keep recording these instances and your list grows longer, observe whether your happiness expands as well.

PROLONGING THE DREAM

Once you've had some practice, you'll be able to tell when the lucid dream is starting to wind up (quite literally, from an inner yoga point of view, as the subtle winds come up). Usually the visual aspects start to change. Images fade and scenes become more disjointed or cartoon-like; the movie is falling apart. The duration of a lucid dream depends on your ability to maintain a balance between dreaming and waking consciousness. It's our "middle way" theme again, like walking a tightrope between these two states. If dreaming consciousness dominates, you'll fall off the rope and into a non-lucid dream. If waking consciousness dominates, you'll wake yourself up.

If you're too loose and find yourself getting sucked into the contents of the dream, thereby losing lucidity, remind yourself, *This is a dream.* Tighten up and get back on the rope. Retreat from the dream a bit; distance yourself from the display. Continue to convince yourself that you're dreaming by doing things you can't do in waking reality, like flying or breathing under water. Engaging in otherworldly activity is like inserting a dreamsign; you're creating a dream event or activity that keeps you clued in to the fact that you must be dreaming.

Going non-lucid (being too loose in your dreams) is just like getting sucked into a daydream or fantasy. You're too involved with the contents of your mind. It's usually movement that sucks you in, like when a good movie draws you into its plot. The faster the movement, the more readily we get sucked in. Action movies suck us in more quickly than slower-paced art films.

EXERCISE: Take Notice

The next time you find yourself drifting off into reverie or fantasy, catch that moment of non-lucidity and step back. Get lucid. The seduction into movement also happens in meditation, in which a single thought can sweep you away into non-lucidity. During meditation, you counteract the seductive power of movement with the stasis of your meditation posture. So this exercise is to similarly "posture" yourself in more of a witnessing mode, to notice the habit of getting sucked into the movement of mind, and to back out.

It's a more refined version of the preceding emotional exercise. Now it's not just charged emotions that we're differentiating from, but the more subtle movement of thought itself. Take notes, here, of how often this happens today, and how far into the "movie" you unconsciously go before you catch yourself and become lucid.

_____

_____

_____

In your lucid dreams, if you're too tight and find yourself backing out too far, or you're about to wake up, step back in. Dive back into the dream content and allow the dream to grab hold of you again. Try rubbing your dream hands together, or spinning your arms like pinwheels, which engages the dream and keeps you in it.

The daily practice here is to allow yourself to step back into a charged emotion and see what that does to your awareness. How quickly do you lose it in non-lucidity? The goal is to go back in and yet retain a sliver of lucidity. Describe your experience of going back into an emotion, but doing so with the intention to sustain lucidity.

_____

_____

_____

_____

EXERCISE: Changing Dream Scenes

If you're in a lucid dream and don't like what's happening or want to change the scene, there are several ways to make the change:

- If your lucidity is strong, you can take control of the dream and make a new scene by willing it to happen.

- Spin like a whirling dervish in your dream and either see where you end up when you stop (it's almost always a different scene) or tell yourself, while you're spinning, that you'll land in a different scene when you stop. This technique also serves to extend the lucid dream if it's starting to fade, akin to spinning your arms like pinwheels, or rubbing your hands.

- To stop the lucid dream altogether, either focus on a single point of a dream scene or close your dream eyes. Holding your dream eyes motionless tends to hold your physical eyes still, which ends the rapid eye movement that defines REM sleep (in which most of our dreams happen) and kicks you out of the dream.

- Closing your dream eyes can sometimes stop a lucid dream. Just for fun, try closing your eyes in your next lucid dream, and see what happens. Write down what you experience.

_____

_____

_____

_____

_____

EXERCISE: Imagine That

Use your imagination to conjure up a scene. For example, imagine that you're in a dark dungeon, or at the bottom of a well. Get into it, in both senses. Feel the slippery slime; smell the mildew. Let yourself get carried away. Then simply change the scene to being at the top of the well, sitting on the rim, or outside of the castle that harbors the dungeon. It's relatively easy to change a scene in your mind like this during the day, but harder when that mind becomes reality at night. But by doing so now, you can grease the skids for doing so then. Is this easy for you, or difficult? Are you able to hold this visualization, or do you get easily distracted?

_____

_____

_____

_____

EXERCISE: Going Back into the Dream

If a dream dissolves and you find yourself awake, don't toss and turn in bed or otherwise move. Movement engages the waking state and draws you into it. Instead:

1. Lie still and dive back into your mind.

2. Imagine that you're spinning or rubbing together the hands of the dream body you just left.

3. Add the resolute intention that you'll soon be dreaming again, and that the dream will be lucid (in the spirit of the MILD technique). (Otherwise, you may end up reestablishing the dream but not recognize it as a dream.) The lucid dream you reenter may not last very long, but that doesn't diminish its validity as a lucid dream.

4. The following morning, try to pick up the scent of the last dream you had by turning your attention back in, then write down what you experience.

_____

_____

_____

_____

Turning your attention within is one way to play with the hypnopompic state (emergence from sleep) and to explore dipping in and out of waking and dreaming consciousness. It's also another way to work with the WILD technique.

Armed with the tips and tricks of these last two chapters, you'll be able to handle any obstacle that you encounter. Once you step onto the tightrope of lucidity and get a feel for the balance between too tight and too loose, you can "high-wire" your way over any hurdle. You will also discover that this type of balance is precisely what makes for good meditation. If you're too loose in meditation, your mind will get soggy and you'll start to doze off on the cushion or get lost in endless thought. If you're too tight, your mind will react like a horse with a saddle that's strapped too tight and buck like crazy. So once again, good meditation leads to good lucidity.

CHAPTER 12

Stages of Lucid Dreaming

With all the techniques presented in part II, sooner or later you will start to have lucid dreams. It's just a matter of time. The next obvious question is, now what? What do you do with these special dreams? It's up to you. Before we continue, write down your hopes and aspirations. When you think about lucid dreaming, what is it that you really want to accomplish? Writing this down will serve as a baseline for how your aspirations may develop.

Many lucid dreamers begin with the entertainment aspects and gradually progress to deeper psychological or spiritual work. This progression can be recapitulated in the context of a single lucid dream. In other words, you can have some fun at the beginning of a lucid dream and then move on to more advanced practices. Play around in the shallow end of the pool. Then, when it feels right, venture to the deep end and take the plunge into more advanced adventures.

Other lucid dreamers will stay at the entertainment level every night. Either progression is fine. What you do also depends on how clear and stable your dreams are and how long they last. At first you might be able to witness only a brief lucid dream and not do much with it. That's still wonderful, a big first step. With patience and perseverance, your dreams will "come true" and gradually stabilize, lengthen, and become clearer, allowing you to do more.

Daily meditation is one of the best ways to augment this stability, durability, and clarity—because dreams are made of your mind. There is no preexisting dreamscape that you plop into every night. It's just your mind in there, expressing itself in a state free from sensory constraint.

EXERCISE: Lucidity in Meditation

Describe your meditation here: how stable, durable, and clear are your sessions? Are you easily distracted and frequently lost in thought, experiencing steadily increasing stretches of lucidity, or something in between?

_____

_____

_____

_____

Everybody begins with meditation that is unstable, foggy, and fragile. That's okay. We start where we are. For the next few weeks, journal how your meditation changes as you establish a regular practice.

_____

_____

_____

_____

_____

_____

_____

_____

What do you notice about your dreams, the more you meditate? Do they change as your meditation matures?

_____

_____

_____

There are no hard metrics for when stability, durability, and clarity will start to blossom in your meditation, just as there are no metrics for when you'll start to have lucid dreams. Progress tends to occur slowly, because most people don't suddenly devote their lives to meditation or to attaining lucidity. This is why journaling is so helpful. With a baseline record, you can look back and see how far you've come.

INTENTION IS THE TICKET

All the opportunities for lucid dream activities I introduced in chapter 3 await you. You can rehearse things, work on interpersonal issues, enhance your sports, meditate, and even prepare for death. As you ponder all these potential activities, which ones stand out for you? Which ones would you like to be able to do? Now is the time to set some goals.

The key to any activity is your intention. After setting the primary intention to wake up in your dreams, set the secondary intention to become lucid *so* that you can fly, have a romantic encounter, practice the piano, or whatever. That second order (in both senses: second *level* as well as second *command*) of intention plants the seed for your nightly adventures. Once you become lucid, reset the intention at the beginning of your lucid dream for what you want to do. *Cool, I'm lucid—now what? Oh yes, tonight I was going to practice the piano in my dream!* And off to the keyboard you go. Prospective memory comes into play yet again as you remember what it was you intended to do after attaining lucidity.

The power of belief underlies the entire journey. Believe, in your bones, that you *can* and *will* become lucid tonight. Believe with all your heart that you *can* accomplish your intentions.

EXERCISE: State Your Intention

1. Set your intention now that you will absolutely, positively become lucid tonight.

2. Pause for a minute, repeat this mantra, and really mean it.

3. Then write down here that you will become lucid so that you can fly in your dreams. (If flying doesn't speak to you, write down what does.)

4. Now ask for more, and be specific. Write down whatever gets you excited, and commit your enthusiasm to paper. Write something like, *Tonight I'm going to become lucid so I can fly through the clouds and plunge like a fighter pilot toward the earth, then soar back up to the heavens!* Put your heart into it; visualize yourself flying through the clouds.

_____

_____

_____

_____

_____

LUCID SLEEP ONSET, REVISITED

While the greatest benefits of lucid dreaming occur in longer dreams, there is plenty that you can explore as a lucid dreamer even as you fall asleep. You can aspire to attain long lucid dreams, knowing all along that taking baby steps is what will get you there. A lengthy lucid dream is like reading an entire chapter in a book, but you can derive insight from a single sentence, or even an appropriately placed word. Seasoned lucid dreamers may not have grand lucid dreams every night, but they practice nightly by working with liminal dreams in the hypnagogic and hypnopompic states I introduced earlier. Working with these "threshold dreams" infuses a heightened sense of awareness into the entire sleeping and dreaming experience.

Pay more attention as you drop into sleep or wake up in the morning. When you're falling asleep, the lotus visualization can help with liminal dreaming because it provides a new background that allows you to better observe your mind as you doze off. It's akin to the daily meditation technique of being mindful of your body and breath, which provides a new background for better observing your mind. Without that contrast, it's harder to see your thoughts. Perception is always generated in contrast. You see these black letters you're reading because they're set against the background of this white page. Meditation techniques often double as contrast media, allowing you to more clearly observe the contents of your mind.

EXERCISE: Exploring Liminal States

Journal (after the fact, not during) what you notice as you fall asleep or when you wake up. Be inquisitive. Do you start to see the gaps between your thoughts as you slip into sleep? Do you dip in and out of these gaps? Write down what you observe.

_____

_____

_____

_____

_____

_____

To help you get oriented in your descent into sleep, researchers have described four stages of hypnagogia: the experience of flashes of light and color, drifting faces and nature scenes, thought-image amalgamations, and hypnagogic dreamlets, or very short dreams. Do you recognize these descriptions as what you experience as you fall asleep? If not, write down what you do experience.

_____

_____

_____

These questions, like many others here, are designed to "lead the witness"—to draw you toward a more lucid relationship to sleep. If you wish, you can try to anchor each of these four stages with the four petals of the lotus visualization—but don't get hung up if this association doesn't work for you.

If you're mindful of the descent into sleep, you can watch thoughts transform into dreams. Because they're usually so brief, it's difficult to do much with these dreamlets, but merely observing them becomes a viable form of liminal dreaming or lucid sleep onset. It's fascinating to watch a thought bubble morph into an image, which in turn morphs into a dream. The bubble quickly pops, as that thought-image-dream evaporates, but almost immediately another thought arises and the process repeats. Remember the adage: thoughts are to waking consciousness as dreams are to dreaming consciousness. By watching the transformation from thought to thought-image to dream-let, you're tracking the transition from waking to dreaming consciousness, a subtle form of WILD. In other words, this tracking process is a way to seed waking-initiated lucid dreams.

You can either watch this progression as a lucid observer without doing anything, or you can try to direct the show by gently holding onto a thought with mindfulness. Then guide that thought into the dream zone (stage four of hypnagogia) using a very delicate intention, and watch it "inflate" into a dreamlet. This inflation is generated by the inner winds, which blow up the thought from a mere thought bubble into a bigger dream bubble. It's a marvelous practice because there is no shortage of material to work with. Thoughts continue to arise, like endless bubbles in a soda, and you continue to watch them inflate into these short lucid dreams.

EXERCISE: Incubate Your Liminal Dreams

Observing your mind in this way can also double as a miniature form of dream incubation. In other words, you can plant a thought intentionally, which then transplants into the dream zone and blossoms into a lucid dreamlet of your specific making. Try it the next time you take a nap or fall asleep. Take the thought of a zebra (or anything else that grabs your fancy), and gently hold it with mindfulness as you doze off. At a certain point, release your mindful grip and let the thought-image-dream go, like an inflated balloon rising into the sky. Later, write down what you noticed.

_____

_____

With practice, anybody can explore these transformations in mental content. At first you might feel like you're just fumbling around in the dark as your mind dips in and out of sleep, and you lose and regain your lucidity. Be patient. You're trying to counteract a lifetime of non-lucid habits. Then journal your experience so that you can track your progress in liminal dreaming:

_____

_____

_____

_____

Because these exercises invite heightened awareness, they also serve to set the stage for lucid dreaming proper.

SAMPLE STAGES

In addition to the nearly infinite opportunities to entertain yourself with lucid dreams or to engage in the many practices associated with the spectrum of benefits discussed earlier (rehearsal, problem solving, working with grief, and so on), here is a fresh sampling of practices you can do once you become lucid. I have selected the following practices because they're relatively accessible and also entertaining. These exercises also point out how "failures" can be viewed as success: the challenges in doing them can point out blind spots. Using the maxim that obstacles are opportunities in disguise, you can learn a great deal about yourself by what you *can't* do in your dreams. This is why I never get discouraged with lucid dreaming. No matter what happens, I'm always learning about myself, bringing unconscious processes into the light of consciousness, and using blind spots to help me to see—which is a big success.

EXERCISE: Make Some Changes

1. Set the intention that the next time you become lucid, you will change the appearances in your dreams. For example, change that dream elephant into a car, that flower into a chair, or that house into a rainbow.

2. A variation is to multiply things in your dreams. Hold your dream hand in front of you and try to add some extra fingers, or make another hand sprout out from your wrist. Or take that dream vase and make two of them.

3. When you wake up, journal what you experienced. Was it easy? Difficult? Impossible? Did it take a long time to accomplish the transformation? Was it easier to transform some objects than others? If you couldn't do it any of it, journal that "failure."

_____

_____

_____

_____

Here's a daytime variation that helps:

1.   Close your eyes, settle your mind with a few deep breaths, and simply notice what pops into your mind. Don't *do* anything; just observe the display.

2.   Now imagine a pink elephant. Hold it in your mind's eye. It helps to scan the pink elephant from trunk to tail, visualizing the ears, perusing its four massive legs, and so on. See if you can do this for at least a minute.

3.   Now flip the color from pink to green, and repeat.

4.   Is this easy or difficult? Write down what you experience.

    _____

    _____

    _____

    _____

5.   Now replace the green elephant with a white jumbo jet. Hold the jet in your mind's eye and scan it back and forth. How did that go?

    _____

The more clear and stable this exercise gets, the more you can transfer this ability into your dreams.

Why do this? What does this practice reveal? First, it's fascinating to watch your dreams morph into different things right in front of your dream eyes. To witness a dream zebra shape-shifting into a piano is right out of a sci-fi movie or video game. It makes you feel like a wizard from the Harry Potter series. Second, this practice develops a sense of mind control. Remember, dream control is essentially self-control, and self-control is essentially mind control. You're becoming the master of your own mind.

By transforming that zebra into a piano in your dreams, you're actually learning how to transform the contents of your mind. This capacity doesn't stay tucked under the blanket of darkness, separate from daily life. In the spirit of bidirectionality, your proficiency in dream transformation will start to appear in daily life, helping you transform solid states of mind. Let's say you're in the midst of an angry outburst when the memory of changing that zebra into a piano pops into your mind, showing you that your anger is not as solid as you think. Anger is essentially as dreamlike, and therefore malleable, as that zebra. This practice will show you that you don't have to fall victim to emotional upheaval. Changing that zebra into a piano at night will show you how to transform anger into empathy, or jealousy into equanimity, or pride into compassion during the day.

EXERCISE: Contemplate Suffering

This exercise is one of the most important in the book.

First, take a moment to reflect on these questions: *Why do you suffer? What is it that makes life so hard?* Before reading the rest of this exercise, contemplate this question and journal your answer. What I will offer has more impact if you search for your own answers first.

_____

_____

_____

_____

_____

_____

_____

Without reflection, there are as many superficial answers as there are difficult life situations. But if you reflect deeply, you will find a common denominator. The main reason we suffer is because we take the contents of our mind and reality to be so solid and real.

Anger causes suffering because we think it's so bloody real. Greed leads to problems because we mistake it to be so solid. Passion leads to pain because we reify it. Lucid dreaming can show you that anger, greed, passion, or any other state of mind is just as ephemeral as a dream. This doesn't deny the appearance of the energy we call anger, greed, or passion, but it does challenge the status of that appearance and reveal its dreamlike nature. When we go along with the appearance of anger and take it to be so real, we're becoming non-lucid to that state of mind. Just as we do in a non-lucid dream, we lose ourselves in the anger, get swept away with it, and suffer the consequences.

For the second step of this exercise, the next time you get angry or upset about something or can't stop worrying about it, take a good look at that state of mind. Look at it the same way you looked at that zebra when you were trying to change it into a piano. What happens when you pause and look directly at that anger? Does anything change? Does the mere act of looking alter your relationship to that thought or emotion? Write down what you experience.

_____

_____

_____

_____

Even if you can't change the zebra or the anger, you're starting to see through it. Just stopping to take a look at these solid states of mind, instead of getting swept away by them, is the practice of lucidity.

This is not an easy exercise, because of the power of the force of habit. Our default is to cave in to the anger and lose ourselves in it. Even our colloquialisms reveal this; we say, "Wow, she really lost it there," or "That guy got totally carried away." Exactly the same process occurs when we get lost in, and carried away by, a non-lucid dream. The point is, *the more solidly you perceive the contents of your mind, the more you will suffer.* A totally "endarkened" or non-lucid relationship to the contents of mind is one way to define psychosis. Everything that occurs in this "dark" mind is so solid, heavy, and painfully real. At the other end of the spectrum, a totally enlightened or fully lucid relationship to the contents of mind is one way to define enlightenment. Everything that occurs in this "lit" mind is light, easy, and free. It's the same mental content, but a totally different relationship.

CUTTING THROUGH APPEARANCES

Most of us live somewhere on the spectrum from beast to Buddha, psychotic to mystic. This spectrum is created by the degree to which we fully identify with, and solidify, the contents of our experience.

EXERCISE: Penetrating Appearances

The next time you find yourself in a lucid dream, try to penetrate the appearances in the dream. For example, if you happen to be in a house, walk up to a dream wall and try to either put your hand through the wall or walk through it. If you're in some open space, try to drop through the ground of your dream. If there's some other object, like a pole or table, see if you can plunge your hand through it. When you wake up, journal what you experienced. Did you bump up against the wall? Were you able to penetrate it at all? If so, did it happen quickly or take some time? Is this easy, difficult, or just impossible for you?

_____

_____

_____

_____

_____

_____

_____

Some people can't do this exercise at first. But the failure is revelatory—and therefore another success. It reveals how solidly you take the appearances of your life, another instance of dreams as truth tellers. This exercise can also expose how part of you wants to feel "walled in" or controlled by external circumstances. It might also reveal that while part of you really does want freedom (the Buddha within you), another part does not (the beast within you that still needs to be caged). Don't judge what you experience. Use these exercises to learn about yourself. Let them point out your blind spots.

Conclusion

In addition to all the lucid dreaming benefits and activities we've already discussed, the practices in this book give you a sense of the limitless potential offered by these remarkable dreams. Lucid dreaming is a pioneering venture, blazing new frontiers in human development. It's on the fringe—but that's exactly where evolution takes place. Neuroscientist and sleep researcher Matthew Walker writes:

> It is possible that lucid dreamers represent the next iteration in Homo sapiens' evolution. Will these individuals be preferentially selected for in the future, in part on the basis of this unusual dreaming ability—one that may allow them to turn the creative problem-solving spotlight of dreaming on the waking challenges faced by themselves or the human race, and advantageously harness its power more deliberately?[38]

The philosopher and paleontologist Teilhard de Chardin proclaimed that consciousness now leads the evolutionary march. Evolution hasn't stopped. It's only moved indoors—the same place we move into when the natural curfew of the night takes us indoors, and then further within as we go to sleep. Lucid dreams are sometimes called *metacognitive* dreams; *meta* means "beyond" or "on top of," so "metacognition" means "thinking about thinking" or "cognition about cognition," becoming aware of one's awareness. Metacognitive dreams are beyond normal dreaming. Lucid dreams suggest a more evolved form of dreaming.

There is a provocative overlap between the regions of the brain that are activated in lucid dreaming (the precuneus, the dorsolateral prefrontal cortex, and the orbitofrontal cortex, all intimately involved in metacognition) and the regions that have expanded the most in recent evolution. The "frontal" edge of evolution is literally represented in these frontal and prefrontal areas of the brain (apes don't have this frontal cortex, which is why their foreheads slope back so abruptly). It's equally compelling that the same regions of the brain are dysfunctional in those with mental disorders characterized by psychosis. So the "psychotic to mystic" spectrum has some neurological footing.

Understanding the pioneering role of lucid dreaming and its cutting-edge place in evolution can inspire us to keep hacking through the underbrush. There's a reason why lucid dreaming is challenging and why trial and error is part of the path to lucidity. That's the way evolution advances. And that's the same way we advance as lucid dreamers. We see what works and what doesn't; we fall down and get back up; we stumble around in the dark, not totally sure where we're going. But as trailblazers interested in personal evolution, we never give up. The view from beyond, the spectacle that is on top of our old way of dreaming, is truly breathtaking. It makes all the hacking worthwhile.

And remember, you're not just doing this for yourself. Lucid dreamers are patiently clearing the way for others to follow. By carving out a path into themselves in the darkness of the night, lucid dreamers are tunneling into the future—and forging a trail for others to follow into the light.

Suggested Reading

Bogzaran, Fariba, and Daniel Deslauriers. *Integral Dreaming: A Holistic Approach to Dreams.* New York: State University of New York Press, 2012.

Brown, David Jay. *Dreaming Wide Awake: Lucid Dreaming, Shamanic Healing, and Psychedelics.* Rochester, VT: Park Street Press, 2016.

Gackenbach, Jayne, and Stephen LaBerge, eds. *Conscious Mind, Sleeping Brain: Perspectives on Lucid Dreaming.* New York: Plenum, 1998.

Garfield, Patricia. *Creative Dreaming.* New York: Ballantine, 1974.

Gyatrul Rinpoche. *Natural Liberation: Padmasambhava's Teachings on the Six Bardos.* Translated by B. Alan Wallace. Boston: Wisdom Publications, 1998.

Hurd, Ryan, and Kelly Bulkeley, eds. *Lucid Dreaming: New Perspectives on Consciousness in Sleep.* 2 vols. Santa Barbara, CA: Praeger, 2014.

Johnson, Clare. *Complete Book of Lucid Dreaming: A Comprehensive Guide to Promote Creativity, Overcome Sleep Disturbances, & Enhance Health and Wellness.* Woodbury, MN: Llewellyn Publications, 2017.

Kingsland, James. *Am I Dreaming? The New Science of Consciousness and How Altered States Reboot the Brain.* London, Atlantic Books, 2019.

LaBerge, Stephen. *Lucid Dreaming: A Concise Guide to Awakening in Your Dreams and in Your Life.* Boulder, CO: Sounds True, 2004.

LaBerge, Stephen. *Lucid Dreaming: The Power of Being Awake and Aware in Your Dreams.* New York: Ballantine, 1985.

LaBerge, Stephen, and Howard Rheingold. *Exploring the World of Lucid Dreaming.* New York: Ballantine, 1990.

Morley, Charlie. *Dreams of Awakening: Lucid Dreaming and Mindfulness of Dream and Sleep.* London: Hay House, 2013.

Namkhai Norbu Rinpoche. *Dream Yoga and the Practice of Natural Light.* Edited and introduced by Michael Katz. Ithaca, NY: Snow Lion Publications, 1992.

O'Flaherty, Wendy Doniger. *Dreams, Illusion, and Other Realities*. Delhi: Motilal Banarsidass, 1997.

Sparrow, G. Scott. *Lucid Dreaming: Dawning of the Clear Light*. Virginia Beach, VA: A.R.E. Press, 1982.

Tenzin Wangyal. *The Tibetan Yogas of Dream and Sleep*. Boston: Snow Lion Publications, 1998.

Thompson, Evan. *Waking, Dreaming, Being: Self and Consciousness in Neuroscience, Meditation, and Philosophy*. New York: Columbia University Press, 2015.

Varela, Francisco J., ed. *Sleeping, Dreaming, and Dying: An Exploration of Consciousness with the Dalai Lama*. Boston: Wisdom Publications, 1997.

Waggoner, Robert. *Lucid Dreaming: Gateway to the Inner Self*. Needham, MA: Moment Point Press, 2009.

Wallace, B. Alan. *Dreaming Yourself Awake: Lucid Dreaming and Tibetan Dream Yoga for Insight and Transformation*. Boston: Shambhala, 2012.

Young, Serinity. *Dreaming in the Lotus: Buddhist Dream Narrative, Imagery, and Practice*. Boston: Wisdom Publications, 1999.

Notes

Endnotes

1   Robert L. Van de Castle, *Our Dreaming Mind* (New York: Ballantine Books, 1995), 457.

2   Marianne Williamson, *A Return to Love: Reflections on the Principles of "A Course in Miracles"* (New York: Harper Collins, 1992), 190–191.

3   Ibid.

4   Melissa Dahl, "People Who Can Control Their Dreams Are Also Better at Real Life," *New York Magazine*, September 11, 2014. https://www.thecut.com/2014/09/lucid-dreamers-are-better-problem-solvers.html.

5   Clare R. Johnson, "Magic, Meditation, and the Void: Creative Dimensions of Lucid Dreaming," in *Lucid Dreaming: New Perspectives on Consciousness in Sleep*, vol. 2: *Religion, Creativity, and Culture*, edited by Ryan Hurd and Kelly Bulkeley (Santa Barbara, CA: Praeger, 2014), 65.

6   Janine Chasseguet-Smirgel, "Creative Writers and Day-dreaming: A Commentary," in *On Freud's Creative Writing and Day-dreaming*, edited by Ethel Spector Parson, Peter Fonagy, and Servulo Figueira (New Haven, CT/London: Yale University Press, 1995), 113.

7   Johnson, "Magic, Meditation, and the Void," 48.

8   Ibid., 65.

9   Daniel Erlacher, "Practicing in Dreams Can Improve Your Performance," *Harvard Business Review*, April 2012. https://hbr.org/2012/04/practicing-in-dreams-can-improve-your-performance.

10   Kelly Bulkeley, "Lucid Dreaming and the Future of Sports Training," *Psychology Today*, May 8, 2015. https://www.psychologytoday.com/us/blog/dreaming-in-the-digital-age/201505/lucid-dreaming-and-the-future-sports-training.

11   Stephen LaBerge, *Lucid Dreaming: A Concise Guide to Awakening in Your Dreams and in Your Life*. (Boulder, CO: Sounds True, 2004).

12   D. T. Jaffe and D. E. Bresler, "The Use of Guided Imagery as an Adjunct to Medical Diagnosis and Treatment," *Journal of Humanistic Psychology* 20 (1980): 45–59.

13   "Some People Are Using Lucid Dreams to Be More Productive While They Sleep," *Business Insider*, August 18, 2014. https://www.businessinsider.com/inside-lucid-dreaming-2014-8/lightbox.

14   Rainer Maria Rilke, *Letters to a Young Poet* (New York: Random House, 1984), 91–91.

15   Stephen LaBerge, *Lucid Dreaming: A Concise Guide to Awakening in Your Dreams and in Your Life* (Boulder, CO: Sounds True, 2004), 58.

16   Namkhai Norbu, *Dream Yoga and the Practice of Natural Light*, edited and introduced by Michael Katz (Ithaca, NY: Snow Lion, 1992), 41, 61.

17   Johnson, "Magic, Meditation, and the Void," 60.

18   B. Alan Wallace, *Dreaming Yourself Awake: Lucid Dreaming and Tibetan Dream Yoga for Insight and Transformation* (Boston, MA: Shambhala Publications, 2012), 132–133.

19   Sergio Magaña, *The Toltec Secret: Dreaming Practices of the Ancient Mexicans* (New York: Hay House, 2014), 47.

20   Johnson, "Magic, Meditation, and the Void," 63.

21   Nicholas D. Kristof, "Alien Abduction? Science Calls It Sleep Paralysis," *New York Times*, July 6, 1999.

22   Michael Finkel, "Want to Fall Asleep? Read This Story," *National Geographic*, August 2018, 66.

23   Matthew Walker, *Why We Sleep: Unlocking the Power of Sleep and Dreams* (New York: Scribner, 2017), 8.

24   Stanford Center for Sleep Sciences, "Exploring New Frontiers in Human Health," *The Stanford Challenge*.

25   Finkel, "Want to Fall Asleep?," 77.

26   Rick Hanson and Richard Mendius, *Buddha's Brain: The Practical Neuroscience of Happiness, Love, and Wisdom* (Oakland, CA: New Harbinger Publications, 2009).

27   Patricia Garfield, *Creative Dreaming* (New York: Ballantine, 1974), 200.

28   Elisabeth Rosen, "Virtual Reality May Help You Control Your Dreams," *Atlantic*, September 15, 2016. https://www.theatlantic.com/science/archive/2016/09/virtual-reality-may-help-you-control-your-dreams/500156/.

29   Ibid.

30   Ibid.

31   Michael Gershon, *The Second Brain: The Scientific Basis of Gut Instinct and a Groundbreaking New Understanding of Nervous Disorders of the Stomach and Intestines* (New York: Harper, 1998).

32   Candace Pert, *Molecules of Emotion: The Science Behind Mind-Body Medicine* (New York: Scribner, 1997), 141.

33   David Jay Brown, *Dreaming Wide Awake: Lucid Dreaming, Shamanic Healing, and Psychedelics* (Rochester, VT: Park Street Press, 2016), 217.

34   S. LaBerge, K. LaMarca, and B. Baird, "Pre-Sleep Treatment with Galantamine Stimulates Lucid Dreaming: A Double-Blind, Placebo-Controlled, Crossover Study," *PLoS ONE* 13, no. 8 (2018): e0201246. https://doi.org/10.1371/journal.pone.0201246.

35   Charles D. Laughlin, *Communing with the Gods: Consciousness, Culture and the Dreaming Brain* (Brisbane, Australia: Daily Grail Publishing, 2011), 65.

36   Ibid., 63.

37   James Kingsland, *Am I Dreaming? The New Science of Consciousness and How Altered States Reboot the Brain* (London: Atlantic Books, 2019), 50.

38   Walker, *Why We Sleep*, 234.

Andrew Holecek is author of several books and scientific papers on lucid dreaming, including *Dream Yoga* and *Dreams of Light*. He is a member of the American Academy of Sleep Medicine, and offers seminars internationally on lucid dreaming, dream yoga, and meditation. Joining modern knowledge from the West with ancient wisdom from the East, his work is intended to wake us up to our full human potential. Holecek lives near Denver, CO.

MORE BOOKS for the SPIRITUAL SEEKER

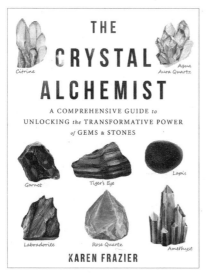

ISBN: 978-1684032952 | US $17.95

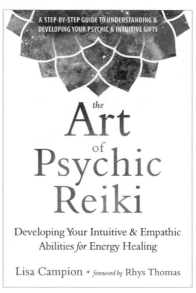

ISBN: 978-1684031214 | US $19.95

ISBN: 978-1684034352 | US $17.95

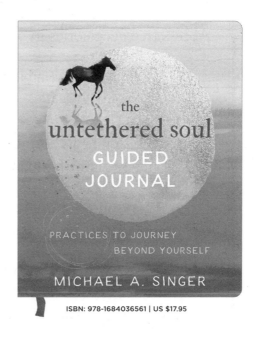

ISBN: 978-1684036561 | US $17.95

newharbingerpublications

REVEAL PRESS

Register your **new harbinger** titles for additional benefits!

When you register your **new harbinger** title—purchased in any format, from any source—you get access to benefits like the following:

- Downloadable accessories like printable worksheets and extra content
- Instructional videos and audio files
- Information about updates, corrections, and new editions

Not every title has accessories, but we're adding new material all the time.

Access free accessories in 3 easy steps:

1. Sign in at NewHarbinger.com (or **register** to create an account).

2. Click on **register a book**. Search for your title and click the **register** button when it appears.

3. Click on the **book cover or title** to go to its details page. Click on **accessories** to view and access files.

That's all there is to it!

If you need help, visit:

NewHarbinger.com/accessories

new harbinger
CELEBRATING
40 YEARS